THE ROBE OF GLORY

An Ancient Parable of the Soul

Born in 1944, John Davidson has had a lifelong interest in mysticism. Graduating from Cambridge University in 1966 with an honours degree in natural sciences, he took a post at the University's Department of Applied Mathematics and Theoretical Physics, where he worked for seventeen years.

While studying for his degree, he came into contact with the teachings of an Indian mystic, and in October 1967 he made the first of many trips to India to meet him.

In 1984, he left the University to pursue other interests. Since then he has written a number of books, including a series on science and mysticism which attempts to demonstrate that all human experience lies within the framework of a greater mystic reality. His particular interest, here, has been to show the true place (and value) of modern science in relation to that reality.

The Robe of Glory is the first in a new series of books planned by the author on the mystic teachings of Jesus and other mystics of his era and culture, including a commentary on the well-known *Song of Songs*.

The Robe of Glory

*An Ancient Parable of
the Soul*

JOHN DAVIDSON

ELEMENT

Shaftesbury, Dorset ● Rockport, Massachusetts
Brisbane, Queensland

© John Davidson 1992

Published in Great Britain in 1992 by
Element Books Limited
Longmead, Shaftesbury, Dorset

Published in the USA in 1992 by
Element, Inc
42 Broadway, Rockport, MA 01966

Published in Australia in 1992 by
Element Books Limited for
Jacaranda Wiley Limited
33 Park Road, Milton, Brisbane 4064

Cover design by James Wasserman
Designed by Roger Lightfoot
Typeset by Colset Pte Ltd, Singapore
Printed and bound in Great Britain
by Dotesios Ltd, Trowbridge, Wiltshire

A catalogue record for this book
is available from the British Library

Library of Congress Catalog Data available

ISBN 1–85230–365–5

CONTENTS

ACKNOWLEDGEMENTS

Thanks are due to the many scholars who have recognized the intrinsic value of this poem, translating it as best they could for our enjoyment and interest – in particular A.A. Bevan, M.R. James and W. Wright. Acknowledgement must also be given to the work of G.R.S. Mead. Writing at the beginning of the twentieth century, Mead devoted much of his life to presenting the early gnostic writings in modern language. In his books, especially *Fragments of a Faith Forgotten*, he collected together much of the gnostic teachings which were available at that time.

Recognition is also due to the many scholars who have translated the other apocryphal and gnostic material quoted. Specifically, to M.R. James (*The Apocryphal New Testament*) and W. Wright (*Apocryphal Acts of the Apostles*) for their translations of the New Testament apocryphal literature; to the team of scholars who contributed to the translations in *The Nag Hammadi Library in English* (1988), edited by J.M. Robinson (quotations reproduced by permission of E.J. Brill); to Bentley Layton for his translations in *The Gnostic Scriptures*; to E.S. Drower for her work on the Mandaean literature, particularly *The Canonical Prayerbook of the Mandaeans* (quotations reproduced by permission of E.J. Brill), and *The Secret Adam* (quotations reproduced by permission of Oxford University Press); to Mary Boyce for her translations of the *The Manichaean Hymn-Cycles in Parthian* (quotations reproduced by permission of Oxford University Press), *On Mithra in the Manichaean Pantheon* and *Sadwes and Pesus*; to Jes P. Asmussen (*Manichaean Literature*), Geo Widengren (*Mani and Manichaeism*) and W.B. Henning (*Brahman*), for their translations of additional Manichaean material; and for their translations of the *Odes of Solomon* thanks are due to J.A. Emerton (quotations from *The Apocryphal Old Testament* reproduced by permission of Oxford University Press), J.H. Bernard, J.H. Charlesworth and J.R. Harris.

Thanks are also extended to Anthea Becker, Miriam Caravella, Julia McCutchen, Beverly Chapman, Valerie Knight, Lionel Metz, K.S. Narang, Santosh Pal, John Rhone, Tom Richman, V.K. Sethi, Faith Singh and Flora Wood, who all went though the manuscript making valuable suggestions. I am also grateful to my good friend Richard Willis who contributed further encouragement and specific insights into the interpretation of the allegory.

But most of all, there are no words to convey the sense of gratitude I feel towards my own dear Master, Maharaj Charan Singh (Radha Soami Satsang Beas, India). Whatever mystical understanding is conveyed in the commentary is due entirely to his grace and blessings. Heartfelt thanks also go out to my Master's successor, Maharaj Gurinder Singh, for his affection, encouragement, counsel and blessing. It is through this association and by reading the writings of other mystics of India and throughout the world, that I have come to see past the obscurity of religion to glimpse the light of the true spiritual reality.

All Masters are one, waves from the Divine Source, and it is a Master who gives a confused and lost soul the key to understanding the simple yet profound, universal yet precise, mystic teachings that are hidden within many of the religious writings of the world, forming the basis of all spiritual teachings. Only by the grace of a perfect living Master – a Living One, as the gnostics called him – can one begin to comprehend the teachings of past Masters. And to be in the service of a perfect Master is the greatest good fortune which can befall any soul.

FOREWORD

Faith Singh

Faith Singh is the daughter of Christian missionary parents. Her mother served as a medical doctor in India in the 1920s and 30s, and her father, the Rt Revd A.O. Hardy, served in India as a priest and then as the Anglican Bishop of Nagpur. The family returned to Britain in the late 1940s and Faith grew up in the UK. She returned to India and settled there when she married an Indian citizen. They live with their three children in Jaipur, India.

I was blessed to be born in a most loving and God-fearing family, whose pivot was the figure of Jesus Christ. By example and precept we absorbed Christ's teachings of love and compassion, of humility and service, of the immanence of the Father throughout the creation, and of the ever-present, guiding hand of His Son. We lived our childhood in the glorious confidence that comes from knowing that we are children of a Father who is all-powerful and all-loving – and that however naughty or confused we may be, we will always be forgiven, we will always have a home.

Then I matured into the world of the mind, of knowledge – of modern scientific knowledge. It spoke to me of dissatisfaction and suffering in spite of progress, of division and strife in spite of communication. Yet all this was supposed to be under the watchful eye of a loving and merciful Father. In my young maturity, I called out to Jesus for answers. I called out for years, but heard no answers. When I needed this guidance, in truth I could not find Him; and though I searched everywhere, I found nothing but my mind. With time I became quiet and sad, and, like the child of the poem, fell into a deep sleep, having partaken indeed of the heavy food of the mind.

When I had given up searching, circumstances brought me into contact with the mystic teachings of a living Master, given in simple, modern language. Within them, I found the answers to all my questions, and I came to understand that there is, in essence, one universal mystic reality, but it is obscured by our minds and often hidden from us by its very simplicity.

Meeting our followers of this mystic way, I realized that we are drawn to a Master by many paths, and from every walk of life and corner of the earth. John Davidson was one of those I came to know. A scientist by training, he has had a lifelong interest in the natural, the scientific and the mystical. In recent years, he has written several pioneering works in 'new science' which deal with the relationships between mind and matter, energy and consciousness, God and the creation. He has drawn on his extensive experience and knowledge of both science and mysticism to put forward answers to many of life's deepest questions. He has also been blessed what is referred to in mystic writings as 'a perfect destiny' – by his coming into contact with a perfect Master, a living Son of God.

In the poem, the Master is the Brother, next in rank to the Father, the King of kings (God Almighty). It is the divine Father who dispatches the letter to the soul – the letter of God's Word, the Holy Spirit – to remind his son, the soul, of his true identity and of the way back to his true home.

The author of the commentary, through his long association with a living Son of God, is able to understand the depth and richness of the mystical allusions contained in the poem. It is a glorious song of reunion – a poem tracing the soul's journey from its divine origin in its royal home, through its sojourn in the world and its time of separation and forgetfulness, to its self-awakening, its realization of its noble heritage, and its final return to its source, the royal king, our Almighty Father.

As I look back on my life, I realize how fortunate I was to

grow up in a Christian family where the essential spiritual content of Christ's teachings was the only thing of real importance. Though we observed the liturgy, and thus lived specifically Christian lives, we tried to understand the nature of the Almighty God for ourselves. It was always made clear that the Lord is in our hearts, and that He is the same loving Father for all mankind.

For those who have set out upon their spiritual journey from within a Christian context and seek to tread the mystic path, *The Robe of Glory* and John Davidson's commentary, will feed the hunger of the spiritual heart. They reinforce our growing understanding of the oneness of all mystical experience; they reinforce our knowledge of the truth.

Faith Singh

And my Letter, my Awakener,
I found before me on the road,
And as with its Voice it had awakened me,
[So] too with its Light it was leading me,
Shining before me in a garment of radiance,
Glistening like royal silk.
And with its Voice and its guidance,
It also encouraged me to speed,
And with his Love was drawing me on.

The Robe of Glory

When I had repeated these words,
With soul a-tremble,
I beheld the Saviour as he shone before me.
I beheld the sight of all the Helmsmen
Who had descended with him to array my soul.
I lifted up my eyes towards that direction
And saw all deaths were hidden by the Envoy.

The Manichaean Hymn-Cycles in Parthian, p.139

INTRODUCTION

The present book is a commentary on an ancient Syriac poem of the early Christian era – *The Robe of Glory*. Found in the 'apocryphal' *Acts of Thomas*, the poem relates the story – in allegorical form – of the soul, sent out from God into the creation, and its eventual return home.

Truth, even if not clearly understood, has a ring to it and many scholars have appreciated the quality of *The Robe of Glory*, with the result that a number of scholarly translations are available. The version used here is mostly that of A.A. Bevan, with the occasional use of other translators – notably W. Wright and M.R. James – whenever Bevan's meaning seemed obscure. To avoid breaking up the text, I have not noted which portions have been taken from Wright and which from James.

The poem is actually written in continuous couplets, but in the interests of clarity and readability, I have divided these up into short 'paragraphs'. A few words have also been added, in brackets, to help clarify the meaning; and in three cases I have ventured a rendering of my own where the translators have admitted their perplexity. These instances are noted in the text.

With regard to the commentary, I do not suggest that my interpretation is correct in all its details. With only scholarly translations to work from and after the lapse of nearly two thousand years, mystical allusions which would probably have been commonplace in those times, now appear obscure. But the general trend and essential meaning would seem to be abundantly clear.

As it appears in the Syriac, the poem is untitled. But by scholars, it has been variously called *The Hymn of the Soul*, *The Hymn of the Robe of Glory* and *The Song of the Pearl*. Here, it is entitled simply, *The Robe of Glory*.

It is not known with certainty who the author was, though some scholars have suggested Bar Daisan, a Syrian mystic who lived in Edessa during the late second and early third centuries. The evidence, however, is so slight that this is little more than conjecture and it would be safer to say that the author is unknown.

Throughout this book and especially in the last four chapters, quotations have been given from other apocryphal and gnostic writings. The translations used for the apocryphal Acts and the *Assumption of the Virgin* are largely from M.R. James's *The Apocryphal New Testament*, being mostly translated from the Greek or Latin. Quotations from his *Acts of Thomas*, however, have been merged, here and there, with a rendering of the Syriac version in W. Wright's *Apocryphal Acts of the Apostles*. The gnostic translations are taken from the revised 1988 edition of *The Nag Hammadi Library in English* (NHL), edited by J.M. Robinson, with some help from Layton Bentley's *The Gnostic Scriptures* (GS).

For the most part, I have been pleasantly surprised at the quality of these scholarly translations. Few scholars have a deep interest and understanding of the mystical path, yet many of the translations still adequately convey the mystic truths intended by the original writers. In places, however, the clarity has been lost, either because the original text itself is corrupt or because the translator could not understand the mystical allusions or technicalities.

In these instances, I have, as in *The Robe of Glory*, either combined the versions of the various translators, lightly editing their rendering, or (very occasionally, when all else failed), substituted a suggested rendering of my own. But the aim has always been one of clarity, whilst remaining faithful to the intended meaning.

1

THE SETTING

SACRED LITERATURE AND ANCIENT DOCUMENTS

For many years, I have read widely amongst the mystic and sacred literature of the world. And like many others who have trod this path, I have been continually impressed, not so much by their diversity, as by the common threads which bind them all. It is true that if one looks at the variety of human interpretations, at the external trappings of the religions who claim these writings as their own, at the differences in the linguistic or cultural modes of expression, or at any other of their more exterior features, one can find differences enough for many a scholarly dissertation and comparison. But if, putting aside all prejudice, one looks with an open mind at the fundamental principles being voiced, one cannot help but note that they are all, essentially, saying the same thing. They all contend that there is one God, or one ultimate Reality, and that He can be found and experienced within each and every individual in an utterly transcendent and indescribable mystic experience.

Whether one reads the *Upanishads*, the *Bhagavad Gita* or the writings of other Indian mystics, ancient or modern; whether one studies the teachings of the Buddha or turns back the clock and searches through what little remains of the original teachings of Zarathushtra; whether one delves into the writings of the Greek or Egyptian mystics or peruses the Quran; whether one reads the poetry of the Sufis of Islam or ponders over the Biblical literature of the ancient Jewish mystics – the same fundamental and simple teachings always seem to be present. And the same is true of the writings to be found in the New Testament, especially those portions of the gospels which can be directly attributed to Jesus.

No doubt the religions which have emerged around these teachings differ, though even they have many fundamental similarities, the one commonly borrowing from its cultural predecessors. Yet, if one looks past the outward accretions of religion to the original teachings, one consistently finds oneself face to face with the same perennial principles.

When, therefore, in more recent years, I turned to an extensive study of the less well-known writings of the early Christian era, I was delighted to find once more the same familiar friends. Indeed, not only are the same truths expressed, but the lyricism of the language is often deeply moving, inspiring and most beautiful.

Many people have the idea, without really considering the matter very deeply, that the few short books to be found in the New Testament are all that remains from the early days of Christianity, and that only the canonical gospels preserve the sayings and teachings of Jesus. Nothing could be further from reality. Early Christian literature actually contains very much more apocryphal than canonical material, reflecting the diversity of thought amongst early Christians, and many of the so-called apocryphal and allied writings are full of the deepest spiritual and mystic truths, with other writing containing clearly mystical elements. It was amongst these that I discovered *The Robe of Glory*, an allegorical poem of such profundity, beauty and completeness, encompassing so many aspects of the mystic path, that I wished to place it before a wider readership at the earliest opportunity.

Since so much unconsidered prejudice surrounds it, it is necessary to say something of the nature and content of the Apocrypha. The term is Latin, being derived from a Greek word meaning 'hidden' or 'secret'. Apocryphal literature stands in contradistinction to canonical writings. Canonical scriptures are those ratified by a high-level council of religious authorities to express accurately the beliefs of their religion.

Apocryphal literature, on the other hand, is characteristically 'deviant' from these beliefs, and frequently considered heretical. In early Christian history, there was often considerable difference of opinion as to what should be decreed canonical. It was by no means a unanimous decision, for example, that the *Gospel According to St John* should be accepted. But both before, and especially after, the institution of the canon, 'orthodox' Christian authorities did their best to eradicate all non-canonical material.

It is because of this stigma of heresy that many people, without ever studying the literature, have a feeling that apocryphal writings are something to be avoided, even shunned. They think, perhaps, that they contain unpleasant or untrue things. This is a greatly limiting point of view, for to approach this ancient literature with an open mind is a rewarding adventure.

It is true that apocryphal writings are often replete with bizarre stories and difficult material. But then, so is much of the New Testament. It was the style of the times. Consider the obscurity of the *Book of Revelation*, for example, or some of the odd stories recounted in Acts and even in the canonical gospels. Familiarity may make these canonical passages and books acceptable, and their contents unquestioned, but does it make them any the more understandable? And how many people can get to grips with the ancient material in the Old Testament? Even the thought processes of those distant writers sometimes seem so different from ours.

The Robe of Glory, itself, is written in Syriac, a Semitic language closely related to Aramaic, and is to be found in the apocryphal *Acts of Thomas*. But its lyrical style differs markedly from the material in which it is embedded, and scholars are agreed that the poem has been written by a hand other than the actual author of these Acts, who no doubt included it because of its charm and beauty.

The unacknowledged incorporation of others' writings into one's own work – with or without significant editorial changes – was a standard practice in ancient times, when all books were individually handwritten and hand-copied. In fact, to really derive the greatest pleasure and benefit from these ancient writings, whether within or without the New

Testament, a little understanding of how ancient books were put together is very helpful.

In dealing with such texts, scholars frequently speak of 'source analysis'. By this they refer to the accepted fact that even books like the four gospels are actually composite documents, put together by some unknown hand from a variety of separate sources which are now mostly lost. This explains, for example, why the *Gospels According to St Matthew* and *St Luke* contain many passages of Jesus's sayings which are identical – word for word – while their narrative elements not only differ widely but are sometimes quite incompatible from a historical point of view. One can compare the differing nativity stories, for instance.

From a 'source analysis' it has been demonstrated many times that the writers of both these gospels had before them a document – now lost – containing Jesus's sayings and parables, a document of pure teachings almost entirely devoid of narrative material. Scholars call it 'Q', from the German *Quelle*, meaning source. The writers then wove these teachings into a narrative sequence according to stories and other teaching material that had been passed on by word of mouth or had been written down at some earlier stage. The *Gospels According to St Matthew* and *St Luke*, for instance, both borrow extensively from the *Gospel According to St Mark*, a text comprised largely of stories, many of a miraculous nature. And Mark, like Luke and Matthew, has itself been analyzed into a number of separate sources.

This editorial procedure on the part of the gospel writers explains why identical sayings and parables commonly appear in completely different settings in Matthew and Luke. Matthew's 'Sermon on the Mount', for example, becomes the 'Sermon by the Seaside' in Luke. It also seems that Luke was concerned about the length of his book, often paraphrasing Jesus's sayings with some detriment to the meaning.

However, this is not the place for a detailed discussion of the content of New Testament writings, which will be deferred to a later book. But a general understanding of how ancient documents were written, together with an awareness of the constant opportunities for editorial tampering to which they have been subjected, explains many of the anomalies, inconsistencies and *non sequiturs* to be found in so much of ancient literature, especially that of a religious nature.

It is only when such factors, together with the ancient mystic writers' love of metaphor and allegory, are borne in mind that the content of the *Acts of Thomas* can be disentangled. For at first sight, the book appears to have been written as a number of quite impossible stories – snakes and wild asses that speak, magical escapes from prison, dead people coming to life and much else besides. Embedded in these tales, however, are some beautiful mystical passages. This is also the case with a number of other apocryphal Acts, though the *Acts of Thomas* is probably the richest in mystical material.

In fact, a closer study of the stories themselves reveals that in many instances they too were once either mystic parables – like Aesop's fables – or were actually written as mystic allegories or anecdotes. Whatever their origin, they were certainly not meant to be taken as real events, but only as metaphors and vehicles for mystic truths. This style of allegorical writing has been characteristic of many mystical writers of the past, especially in the East.

The unknown author of the *Acts of Thomas* gives these stories their pseudo-historical setting by weaving them around one of Jesus's apostles, Judas Thomas and his mission to India. Some of the stories he has probably invented, others have been drawn from various traditions and modified to suit his own purposes and bent of mind, adding material of his own or from other sources, as he saw fit. And the whole may also have undergone editing by later copyists with varying points of view, thereby adding further confusion.

Fortunately, many of the 'speeches', 'songs', 'prayers' and spiritual discourses, many seeming to stem from other writers, have been retained either intact or with very little modification. For it was clearly one of the writer's intentions to present these mystical passages, though in a setting differing considerably from that in which he had found them. And it is in one of these passages that we find *The Robe of Glory*, said – in the *Acts of Thomas* – to have been sung by Judas Thomas whilst in captivity in India.

GNOSTIC WRITINGS

The Robe of Glory is no isolated example of the use of allegory in ancient mystic literature. It is part of a rich heritage of those times, a tradition found mostly in the gnostic and apocryphal writings, and providing part of the backdrop, not only to *The Robe of Glory*, but also to the New Testament and to all of Jesus's teachings. It is actually a lost or forgotten part of our Christian heritage.

The word *gnosis* means knowledge, and in particular mystic knowledge – an inner, revealed knowledge of God and the workings of His creation. It is an understanding which stems from direct mystic experience rather than intellectual analysis. The differentiation between gnostic and apocryphal literature is often largely academic, for many of the apocryphal writings and gospels are gnostic in nature. Indeed, there is much in the canonical literature which is in accord with so-called gnosticism. And the gnostics themselves frequently gave a mystical interpretation to the 'canonical' sayings of Jesus.

The *Pistis Sophia*, for instance, is a gnostic writing. Yet five of the apocryphal *Odes of Solomon* together with twenty of the canonical psalms are reproduced in it, each being provided with a mystic commentary. And a mystic interpretation is also given to some of the canonical sayings and parables of Jesus.

The designations of canonical, apocryphal and gnostic are therefore all later divisions, given by scholars and theologians. The original writers themselves were simply writing what they considered to be the truth, with little or no thought as to their later historical and religious fate. Even the canonical literature was not designated as such until two hundred years or so after the departure of Jesus.

Little remains of what must once have been a considerable body of diverse gnostic literature, and until the present century our largest sources of information on the gnostics came from the unreliable and biased accounts given by a few of the early church fathers, whose intention was to castigate and pillory rather than to understand. Now that some of the older gnostic writings have been recovered, we are in a better position to gauge the inaccuracies and misrepresentations of their heresy-hunting intolerance.

One zealous bishop, Hippolytus, even undertook to write a synopsis and refutation of every 'heresy' of which he knew. Beginning with the Greeks – Pythagoras, Plato, Aristotle, Democritus, Heraclitus and many others – taking in the ancient beliefs of the Chaldaeans, the Egyptians, the Zoroastrians and the Druids, alighting with relish upon the host of Christian sects he considered unorthodox, and even taking a side-swipe at the Indian Brahmins, Hippolytus presents us with the perfect image of an opinionated and self-righteous mind blindly lashing out at anybody who had ever dared to think differently from himself! He dismisses the entire works of Plato, for example, in no more than five pages, Aristotle faring no better with little more than half a page.

Apart from the interest in studying such a mind at work, Hippolytus is most frustrating. For it is clear that concerning the philosophies and teachings that he ridicules, he is poorly informed, understands but little, and represents with flagrant inaccuracy. Knowledge of those he pillories is thus gained mostly by inference.

There were also other famous fathers who wrote voluminously along similar lines, notably St Irenaeus, Epiphanius, Tertullian and St Ephraim. But from them all we can glean little that is completely trustworthy, though much that is tantalizing.

So 'well' had the suppressors and destroyers of ancient literature done their work, that before the present century hardly a dozen gnostic tractates (short treatises) had been discovered, and these are of considerable interest. But in December 1944, in the Nag Hammadi region of upper Egypt, two brothers came upon a sealed jar whilst digging out nitrogenous earth to fertilize their fields. Inside were twelve ancient leather-bound *codices* or books, whose leaves were made of papyrus. The subsequent fate of these ancient books, preserved for over fifteen centuries in the desert sands, has been told many times in the various books on gnosticism. Its ending, however, was mostly happy, for eleven of these books and the fragmentary remains of the twelfth, now reside in the

Coptic Museum in Cairo. A few leaves from a further book
were also found, slipped inside one of the covers. But the
archaeological and antiquarian heart bleeds when one hears
that the sad condition of the twelfth book is because it was
used as kindling by the mother of the two brothers.

These twelve books, now known as the Nag Hammadi
library, contain a total of fifty-two gnostic tractates, of which
six are duplicates and six were already extant at the time of
the find, including a brief excerpt from Plato's *Republic*. Of
the forty new tractates, about thirty are in a state of good or
reasonable preservation, the remaining ten being somewhat
fragmentary.

The language of the Nag Hammadi library is Coptic, an
Afro–Asian language, descended from ancient Egyptian, but
written in the Greek alphabet. The frequent use of trans-
literated Greek words, however, together with characteris-
tically Greek phraseology and construction, make it clear that
the Coptic is mostly a translation from the Greek.

Although all the tractates are concerned with the mystical
traditions of the times, they appear to vary considerably in
their origins. Some may be pre-Christian, while others
are certainly post-Christian, for Jesus is mentioned or
quoted.

The actual date in which the books were bound can be
gauged fairly accurately from the scrap papyrus – old letters,
invoices and business documents – used to thicken their
leather covers. One of these covers contained documents
dated AD 341, 346 and 348, giving us an earliest date for the
binding of that book.

Various other evidence, including the persecution of
'heretics' by Christian archbishops, leads us to the assumption
that the books were probably buried for safe-keeping,
perhaps for posterity, during the late fourth or early fifth
century. In AD 367, for instance, Athanasius, Archbishop of
Alexandria, wrote an Easter letter to his 'flock', condemning
heretics "and their apocryphal books". Obviously, he had
'problems' in his area! And early in the fifth century,
Shenoute, Abbot of the White Monastery in upper Egypt,
threatened a local group of 'heretics': "I shall make you
acknowledge . . . the Archbishop Cyril, or else the sword will

wipe out most of you, and moreover those of you who are
spared will go into exile" (*NHL p. 20*).

How, one wonders, was such action justifiable in the name
of Jesus, who taught nothing but humility, service and love
towards God and one's fellow man? In the earliest days
of their religion, the Christians, together with many other
'misfits', were persecuted by the Roman authorities. But
dating from the Emperor Constantine's conversion, early in
the fourth century, Christianity was adopted as the state
religion of the Roman Empire, giving the Christian authori-
ties increasing worldly and religious authority. In the absence
of a living teacher and the correct practices of meditation,
mystic teachings are rapidly misinterpreted, externalized and
literalized. They are no longer taken as the guide to an inner
reality which is to be experienced, but are seen as an end,
complete in themselves. And when organization and a sense
of power over others begins to take over, the remaining
vestiges of true spirituality soon evaporate.

Finds such as the Nag Hammadi library rapidly become the
centre of political, religious and academic dispute. There is no
doubt that some modern Christians would happily have seen
the codices forgotten or even burned, like so many books of
antiquity. And scholars can be deeply possessive over access
to manuscripts which could make their name and fame.
Political considerations also come into play when archaeolo-
gical finds are sold or smuggled out of a country.

The end result is delay, and the first tractate to be
published, the *Gospel of Thomas*, did not appear in English
until 1959, while the first English translation of all the
tractates, *The Nag Hammadi Library in English*, was not
published until 1977. Reading through these translations, one
realizes that the real work of actually understanding the texts
has hardly begun. There is little doubt that the translations,
sometimes almost entirely obscure, will require considerable
revision as their meaning becomes more clear.

The above, then, provides some brief background to *The
Robe of Glory* and the other texts used in this book. And
after the commentary on *The Robe of Glory*, the last four
chapters present just a sample of these many and varied
gnostic and apocryphal writings, inasmuch as they echo the

symbolism and teachings of *The Robe of Glory*. And in all of them we find expression of the same eternal and universal truths.

Firstly, however, let us direct attention to *The Robe of Glory*.

2

THE POEM

The Robe of Glory

When I was a little child
And dwelling in my kingdom, in my Father's house,
And in the wealth and the glories
Of my nurturers had my pleasure,
From the East, our home,
My parents, having equipped me, sent me forth.

And of the wealth of our treasury
They had tied up for me a load.
Large it was, yet light,
So that I might bear it unaided –
Gold of Beth-Ellaye,
And silver of Gazzak the great,
And rubies of India,
And agate from the land of Kushan [Africa].
And they girded me with adamant
Which can crush iron.

And they took off from me the bright robe,
Which in their love they had wrought for me,
And my purple toga,
Which was measured and woven to my stature.
And they made compact with me,
And wrote it in my heart,
So that it should not be forgotten:

"If thou goest down into Egypt,
And bringest the one pearl,
Which is in the midst of the sea
Hard by the loud-breathing serpent,
[Then] shalt thou [again] put on thy bright robe
And thy toga, which is laid over it,
And with thy Brother, our next in rank,
Thou shalt be heir in our kingdom."

I quitted the East [and] went down,
There being with me two guides,
For the way was dangerous and difficult,
And I was young to tread it.

I passed the borders of Maishan,
The meeting place of the merchants of the East,
And I reached the land of Babel,
And I entered the walls of Sarbug.
I went down into Egypt,
And my guides parted from me.

I betook me straight to the serpent,
Hard by his dwelling I abode,
[Waiting] till he could slumber and sleep,
And I could take my pearl from him.

And when I was single and alone,
A stranger to those with whom I dwelt,
One of my race, a free-born man,
From among the Easterns, I beheld there –
A youth fair and well-favoured,
And he came and attached himself to me.
And I made him my intimate,
A comrade with whom I shared my merchandise.

And he warned me against the Egyptians
And against consorting with the unclean;
For I had put on a garb like theirs,

Lest they should insult me
Because I had come from afar,
To take away the pearl,
And lest they should arouse the serpent against me.

But in some way or other
They perceived that I was not their countryman.
And with guile they mingled for me a deceit
And I tasted of their food.

I forgot that I was a son of kings,
And I served their king;
And I forgot the pearl,
For which my parents had sent me,
And by reason of the heaviness of their food,
I fell into a deep sleep.

But all those things that befell me,
My parents perceived and were grieved for me;

And a proclamation was made in our kingdom,
That all should speed to our gate,
Kings and princes of Parthia
And all the great ones of the East.
So they wove a plan on my behalf,
That I might not be left in Egypt,

And they wrote to me a letter,
And every noble signed his name thereto:

"From thy Father, the King of kings,
And thy Mother, the Mistress of the East,
And from thy Brother, our next in rank,
To thee our son, who art in Egypt, greeting!
Up and arise from thy sleep,
And listen to the words of our letter!
Call to mind that thou art a son of kings!

See the slavery – [and] whom thou servest!
Remember the pearl

For which thou didst speed to Egypt!
Think of thy bright robe,
And remember thy glorious toga,
Which thou shalt put on as thine adornment.
Thy name is named in the book of life,
And with thy Brother, whom thou hast received,
Thou shalt be in [shalt return to] our kingdom."

And my letter [was] a letter
Which the King [as ambassador
Had] sealed with his right hand,
To keep it from the wicked ones, the children of Babel,
And from the tyrannous demons of Sarbug.

It flew in the likeness of an eagle,
The king of all the birds;
It flew and alighted beside me,
And became all-speech.

At its voice and the sound of its rustling,
I started and arose from my sleep.
I took it up and kissed it,
And loosed its seal, [and] read;
And according to what was traced on my heart
Were the words of my letter written.

I remembered that I was a son of kings,
And my free soul longed for its natural state.
I remembered the pearl,
For which I had been sent to Egypt.

And I began to charm him,
The terrible loud-breathing serpent.
I hushed him to sleep and lulled him to slumber
By naming the name of my Father upon him,
And the name of our next in rank
And of my Mother, the Queen of the East;
And I snatched away the pearl,
And turned to go back to my Father's house.

And their filthy and unclean garb
I stripped off, and left it in their country,
And I took my way straight, to come
To the Light of our home, the East.

And my letter, my awakener,
I found before me on the road,
And as with its voice it had awakened me,
[So] too with its light it was leading me,
Shining before me in a garment of radiance,
Glistening like royal silk.
And with its voice and its guidance,
It also encouraged me to speed,
And with his love was drawing me on.

I went forth, passed by Sarbug,
I left Babel on my left hand,
And reached Maishan the great,
The haven of the merchants,
That sitteth on the shore of the sea.

And my bright robe which I had stripped off,
And the toga wherein it was wrapped,
From the heights of Hyrcania,
My parents sent thither,
By the hand of their treasurers,
Who in their faithfulness could be trusted therewith.

But I remembered not the brightness of it;
For I was yet a child and very young,
When I had left it in the palace of my Father.
On a sudden as I faced it,
The garment seemed to me like a mirror of myself.
I saw in it my whole self,
Moreover I faced my whole self in facing it.
For we were two in distinction,
And yet again one in one likeness.

And the treasurers also,
Who brought it to me, I saw in like manner,

That they were twain [yet of] one likeness.
For there was written on them [both],
The sign of the One King,
By Whose Hand, through them, were restored to me
My treasure and my wealth
And my bright embroidered robe,
Which was variegated with bright colours;
With gold and with beryls,
And rubies and agates
And sardonyxes varied in colour.
And skilfully worked in its home on high,
With diamond clasps, all its seams were fastened;
And the image of the King of kings
Was depicted in full all over it,
And like the sapphire stone also were its manifold hues.

Again I saw that all over it
The instincts [first beginnings] of knowledge [gnosis]
   were stirring,
And as if to speak I saw it also making itself ready.

[Then] I heard the sound of its voice,
Saying, "This thou art;
And for my sake it is that the treasurers have raised you,
To usher you into the presence of my Father."

And I also perceived in myself
That my stature was growing
According to his [their?] labours.

And in its kingly motions
It was spreading itself out towards me,
And in the hands of its givers
It hastened that I might take it.

And love urged me on,
That I should run to meet it and receive it;
And I stretched [myself] forth and received it,
With the beauty of its colours I adorned myself
And in my royal robe excelling in beauty
I arrayed myself, wholly.

I clothed myself therewith, and ascended
To the gate of salutation and homage;
I bowed my head and did homage
To the Majesty of my Father who had sent it to me,

For I had done his commandments,
And he too had done what he had promised.

And at the gate of his princes
I mingled with his nobles;
For he rejoiced in me and received me,
And I was with him in his kingdom.
And with the voice all his servants glorify him.

And he promised that also to the gate
Of the King of kings I should speed with him,
And bringing my gift and my pearl
I should appear with him before our King.

3

THE COMMENTARY

THE STORY OF THE SOUL

The Robe of Glory relates the most ancient of stories – the oldest story ever told – for it tells the tale of the soul's separation from its Eternal Home, in the bosom of the Father, its wanderings in the labyrinth of creation, its follies and its heartaches, its eventual rescue by a divine Messenger sent by the Father, and its final return Home.

In the mythology of every culture and country, in the folklore and fairy tales of every nation, in the mystical allegories of every people, variations of this same story are told. And it is a tale which never fails to captivate, bringing tears to many an eye, for it touches us deep in our spiritual heart, awakening memories of a peace and inner comfort long forgotten, stirring up a longing for the pure realms of being, beyond the strife and turbulence of the material universe.

It is the parable of the Prodigal Son; the Prince who awakens the Sleeping Beauty; or the Princess who has fallen under the spell of an evil power and awaits the touch and mystic kiss of the ever-youthful and life-giving Prince, before her release can be effected.

It is a story, too, which will never cease to be told for as long as the creation continues, for souls – having long ago left their home – will never be at peace in the material realms. The soul separated from its Divine Source is ever restless, finding no peace until reunited with its divine essence.

At all times and in all ages, there have been souls whose inner fires have been set alight, who have been called to make the journey home. And at all times and in all ages, there are divine Messengers, Sons of God, perfect Masters who are sent to guide such souls on their long journey homewards. Indeed, it is the Master, calling from hidden places within the inner realms of Light, who awakens the soul and fills it with desire to find its God, its source of being. But at the outset, the soul does not know who it is that is beckoning – or even that it is being drawn. Like a man waking from a deep slumber, he does not know that there is someone else who is awakening him.

The Robe of Glory, then, tells this ancient tale.

THE HOME OF THE SOUL

When I was a little child
And dwelling in my kingdom, in my Father's house,
And in the wealth and the glories
Of my nurturers had my pleasure,
From the East, our home,
My parents, having equipped me, sent me forth.

Mystics of all ages and cultures have said that the soul is a part of God. If He is an Ocean, they say, then the soul is a drop. If He is Light, the soul is a ray. If He is Fire, the soul is a spark. There can be no closer relationship than that of a drop to the ocean or of a ray to the sun. The Lord is an Ocean of love and bliss. Consequently, the relationship of the soul to the Lord is one of love. Such love involves complete faith and dependence upon the object of that love, and in order to portray this to us mystics have described it in terms of human relationships. Jesus and many other mystics of those times spoke of the Lord as the Father, and the soul as the son. In the parable of the wise and foolish virgins, Jesus also spoke of the meeting of the souls with the Lord as a wedding – a meeting with the Bridegroom – where the feeling is primarily one of love.

Other mystics have spoken of the relationship of the soul
with the Lord as that of a mother to her son, where once again
the bond is one of love. In this poem, Bar Daisan – let us
suppose that it was he – compares the soul to a little child. A
child is entirely dependent upon his parents' care and love,
knowing no other way in which to live.

The child – the soul – dwells in his own kingdom, in the
Father's house. This then, being in the lap of the Father, is the
true and real home for a soul. Moreover, the soul dwells in its
own kingdom, that is: the soul is a king – as well as a little
child.

In this state, the soul rests comfortably in the spiritual
wealth and radiant glory of "my nurturers" – those who
support and give life to a soul – that is, the Lord Himself, the
source of all being. The Lord is the Ocean of Being while the
soul is a drop of that same Ocean. In reality, then, the soul
and the Lord are one.

The poet continues, "From the East, our home . . ." This
poem makes frequent allusions which would have been
commonplace and well-understood by the mystically-minded
of those times. In this instance, "the East" is clearly stated to
be symbolic of "home" – that is, of God, the kingdom of the
soul.

The "East" is an apt metaphor, for that is the side from
which the sun arises, the horizon over which light pours at
the awakening of a new day. Similarly, to the mystics of
those times, God was also known as the Great Light or the
Virgin Light. Seeking a parallel in this world, they therefore
describe God as the "East" – the side from which the light
comes.

THE JOURNEY OF THE SOUL –
AND ITS GARMENTS

From the East, our home,
My parents, having equipped me, sent me forth.

So the "parents" "equip" the soul for a journey away from the
Lord. Since there is nothing which is ever truly away from

the Lord, the 'journey' actually means going out into the Lord's creation – though He is still present in each and every particle of His creation. It is all His projection or His emanation.

The "parents" are the Lord and His creative emanation – the Word or Logos. It is this mystic Word of God which has created the creation and constantly maintains it in existence. The Word is the essence of everything we see around us. It is the Vibration which maintains existence. It is also the essence and inward reality of our own true being, our soul. In other mystic writings, the Word is also called the Name of God or the Son of God, born of the pure and Virgin Light of the Lord.

The necessary 'equipment' for such a journey is the vestures, garments, veils or coverings which the soul needs in its contact with the different spheres of creation. These coverings are required in order that the soul may function within each of the mystic mansions of creation. As Jesus said, "In my Father's house are many mansions. If it were not so, I would have told you" (*St John 14:2*). In the physical realm, we have a gross physical body and a human mind for functioning here. Similarly, we have corresponding minds and bodies, of a more subtle character, for our existence in the higher realms of the Lord's great creation. Mind and body – whether physical, astral or causal – constitute the coverings over the soul that keep it away from God and permit it, or force it, to remain in the creation[1].

The poet continues:

> And of the wealth of our treasury
> They had tied up for me a load.
> Large it was, yet light,
> So that I might bear it unaided –
> Gold of Beth-Ellaye,

---

[1] These regions and coverings can be described in greater details. See glossary for brief details of astral and causal planes. Further information can be found in Dr Johnson's book, *The Path of the Masters*, and other mystic literature. *See* Bibliography.

> And silver of Gazzak the great,
> And rubies of India,
> And agate from the land of Kushan [Africa].
> And they girded me with adamant
> Which can crush iron.

"From the wealth of our treasury" means that the load came from the treasury of the Lord, that is, from the Lord Himself. "Treasury" and "treasure" are terms often encountered in other mystic or gnostic literature of this period. A perfect Master is sometimes known as the Treasurer, for example, whilst God Himself has been described as the Treasury of Light, and many mystics have spoken of "spiritual wealth" and "inner treasures". In the Sermon on the Mount, Jesus also says:

> Lay up for yourselves treasures in heaven. . . .
> For where your treasure is,
> There will your heart be also.

> *St Matthew 6:19, 21*

So the soul is given its coverings, coverings which it is capable of bearing "unaided" – that is, on its own – for the descent into creation entails the increasing isolation of the soul from the Lord and consequently from the rest of His creation. The "load" is also "large . . . yet light". "Large" enough to cover the soul, yet "light" enough for the soul to carry, for the soul is never extinguished by its descent into the creation, however much it may be burdened.

In the poem, this descent is conveyed by the decreasing purity and value of the "load" or coverings: gold, silver, rubies, agate and adamant. The "gold from Beth-Ellaye", the "silver of Gazzak the great" and so on, therefore refer to the stages in creation where the different coverings are taken on, "Gazzak" meaning strength. The last covering is of "adamant" – a garment "which can crush iron". Adamant is a legendary stone, said to be unbreakable and impenetrable. Such a hard and unyielding garment can only be referring of the covering of the physical body, where the soul's isolation is complete. Indeed, in our own language, adamant has come to mean one who is stubborn and unyielding, surely the state of mind of one who is thoroughly separated from God. Over the ages, mystics have used many means of describing the realms of creation. Later, we shall see how the mystic journey through the creation is also likened to a trade route.

The poet's use of "Beth-Ellaye" derives from the mystical heritage of the times. He seems to be alluding obliquely to the book of *Genesis*, said by many mystics of both Jewish and other cultures to be allegorical in nature. There one reads of the ascent of the soul, up from the physical universe to its original home:

> And Abram went up out of Egypt . . .
> And he went on his journeys . . .
> Even unto Beth-El,
> Unto the place where his tent had been at the
>   beginning,
> Between Beth-El and Hai;
> Unto the place of the altar,
> Which he had made there at the first:
> And there Abram called on the name of the Lord.
>
> *Genesis 13:1, 3*

"Egypt", as we shall see, was a metaphor commonly used by mystics of those times for the physical universe. So Abram sets out upon the mystic journey. He travels out of the body, away from the physical universe and comes, "To the place where his tent had been at the beginning." "His tent" means his home, where nomadic people of what we now call the Middle East used to live. It refers to his origin, his source. So Abram returns from the physical universe to his original home, "Where he had been at the beginning;" that is, before he had separated from God. And where was this original home? "Between Beth-El and Hai." Here, unmistakably, is the origin of our poet's "gold of Beth-Ellaye".

And here, too, Abram finds the "altar", the innermost holy of holies, the mystic Source, where he can worship the true

Name of the Lord: the Word or Logos. Moreover, in the Hebrew text, *Beth* means house, *El* is an epithet of God, while *Hai* means life or living. "Beth-Ellaye" thus means 'the house of the Living God', referring to the kingdom of God, the true home of the soul, the mystic Source of life.

So, in the poem, the "gold of Beth-Ellaye" is the innate spirituality and deep devotion of the soul dwelling in the kingdom of God.

> And they took off from me the bright robe,
> Which in their love they had wrought for me,
> And my purple toga,
> Which was measured and woven to my stature.

The process of coming to the nether pole of the creation of necessity means that the "bright robe" of pure spirituality, woven by the love of the soul's parents, is removed, or as other mystics have explained it, covered. Mystics say that the soul in all its naked glory carries with it a resplendent light, but that this light is obscured by the wrappings of creation, like a glowing light with many black cloths around it. Jesus also spoke of the light of the soul and its coverings when encouraging his disciples to be living examples of his teachings, to realize the light of the soul within themselves and to let it pervade all they did. He said:

> Ye are the light of the world.
> A city that is set on an hill cannot be hid.
>
> Neither do men light a candle,
> And put it under a bushel, but on a candlestick;
> And it giveth light unto all that are in the house.
>
> Let your light so shine before men,
> That they may see your good works,
> And glorify your Father which is in heaven.

St Matthew 5:14–16

Repeating his metaphor, the poet adds that the soul's "purple toga" – a royal garment – is also removed, signifying that the child, the soul, is of royal birth, the son of God. In olden times, purple was a precious dye and only royalty had the prerogative to wear it. So if the soul carried with it the full brilliance of its 'royal' magnificence upon its descent into the lower realms, its origin would immediately be known. Therefore, as it descends, the soul has to be increasingly hidden, its garment of light is taken away from it to avoid recognition both by itself and by others. Without this, the divine play of creation could not continue, for all souls would wish to return to God. And if the Lord wishes the creation to continue, there have to be souls in it. It is the Lord, therefore, who sends the souls out – and the Lord who calls them back.

This toga, it can be noted, was "woven to my stature"; that is, it was a well-fitting garment. The only "garment" which fits a soul so perfectly is that of the soul's own innate quality – that of love for the Lord. Love is the most fitting garment for a soul. So "well-fitting" is this "garment" that it is part of the soul itself.

"Garments" and "wedding garments" are common mystical metaphors of the Middle East, both of this period and later. Jesus himself used them, as is recorded in the gospels. In St Matthew's gospel, for example, he tells the tale of many poor people (the souls, depicted as poor travellers in this world) being taken from the highways and from the wayside and being invited by a king (the Lord or Master) to a wedding feast (the inner union of the soul with the Lord). But:

> When the king came in to see the guests,
>   he saw there a man which had not on
>   a wedding garment:
>
> And he saith unto him:
> "Friend, how camest thou in hither
>   not having a wedding garment?"
> And he was speechless.

St Matthew 22:11–14

Here, the "wedding garment" symbolizes the brightness and glory of the pure soul, and its love and devotion for the Lord, without which the divine wedding or union can never be consummated. It is the "bright robe" and the "purple toga" of the poem, the divine garments of the soul. But of these, it is never really divested, only covered.

The poet also says that the "bright robe" and the "purple toga" are gifts from the soul's parents – meaning the Lord. Love and light are the essential qualities of the Lord. They are His gift to a soul. He has made the soul out of His own essence; it is made of love and light, so to speak. Or one can say that love and light are the primary attributes of the Lord and that the soul is a drop of these qualities. There are many ways to express this reality.

THE QUEST FOR THE PEARL

And they made compact with me,
And wrote it in my heart,
So that it should not be forgotten:
"If thou goest down into Egypt,
And bringest the one pearl,
Which is in the midst of the sea
Hard by the loud-breathing serpent,
[Then] shalt thou [again] put on thy bright robe
And thy toga, which is laid over it,
And with thy Brother, our next in rank,
Thou shalt be heir in our kingdom."

This short portion of the poem tells, in a nutshell, the entire story of creation. The parents making "compact" with the soul demonstrate that the creation, and the condition to which the soul has fallen on coming here, is entirely of the Lord's design. The parents *sent* the soul forth. It is the Lord's doing, however strange it may appear to us.

The parents say – or the Lord 'decrees' – that the purpose of the soul's journey into the creation – and in particular into "Egypt", the physical realm – is to find the "one pearl, which is in the midst of the sea, hard by the loud-breathing serpent".

This, then, is the purpose of human life, the purpose of taking a human birth. The pearl is the gnosis – spiritual enlightenment or true knowledge of God. The pearl is also the life force or soul – the essence of God within us all. The "sea" is another commonly-occurring gnostic image, used as a metaphor for the ocean of the material universe, which is constantly swept up into storms and tempests of unrest, darkness and death. "Hard by" the sea is the "loud-breathing serpent". This refers to the impulses, attachments and desires of our ever-active human mind, influenced by the passions, the senses and desire for activity in the world – whether apparently good or bad.

If we consider it, we will see that we do nothing in this world but under the influence of our mind. And the mind is never still. It is constantly on the go – "loud-breathing". Just as you cannot ignore a person who is breathing loudly in your ear, so also are we unable to ignore our mind. All desires and plans are in the mind. All actions are preceded and accompanied by mental activity, however fleeting. Under the influence of the mind, man is loving, generous and kind or he is mean, angry, lustful and egocentric. But in either case, he is deeply involved in the affairs and attachments of physical living. Indeed, at this physical level, our very sense of self is lodged in the mind. This is certainly a "loud-breathing" serpent which gives us no peace or happiness while so deeply bound up in the "sea" of the material world!

Moreover, the mind, being so active and materially inclined never gives a thought to the pearl, to spiritual enlightenment, to the soul or life force which gives us life and being.

Yet, says the poem, the parents of the soul "wrote it in my heart" that their purpose would never be completely forgotten. This refers to the fact that the soul never really forgets its divine origin. It is a part of the divine design. If we sit quietly by ourselves and look honestly within ourselves, we will find that there is always a feeling of something missing. Even if we have every comfort of the world – a good and harmonious family life, a beautiful house, a job we enjoy and so on – even then, if we sit quietly and allow our innermost feelings to surface we will find that there is a sense of

something missing. This is the natural longing of the soul
for its own region, its own kingdom, its real home with
God.

So when this pearl of spiritual enlightenment is found, then
again will the "bright robe" and the "purple toga" be worn
– then again can the soul wear its own natural garment.

But, say the "parents" most significantly, this condition will
be attained, "with thy Brother, our next in rank". It means
that by the decree of the "parents", the soul can only return
to its divine home with the help of a Brother, a perfect Master.
It is only through a perfect Master that the soul can once again
become "an heir in our kingdom" – a true son of his parents,
a true son of God. A perfect Master is one with the Word.
He is a personification of the Word, and in many other
instances in the mystic writings of this period the Master is
also called the Son of God, as well as the Brother. In this
poem, however, the soul is the son and the Master is the
Brother.

The use of the pearl as a mystic metaphor is of interest.
Its very origin lends itself to imagery, for a pearl is found
concealed amongst the flesh of the tightly closed oyster. One
would never suspect the otherwise unbecoming and barnacled
oyster of possessing such a secret treasure. Nor indeed is
the oyster aware of the wealth hidden within itself. So the
parallels to the condition of the divine soul, caught or veiled
by the layers and folds of mind and body, present a rich
harvest for poetic metaphor, and the translucent beauty of the
pearl was commonly used by the mystics of this period to
symbolize the soul and the spiritual goal. St Matthew's gospel
preserves one such example:

> The kingdom of heaven is like unto a merchant man,
> Seeking goodly pearls:
> Who, when he had found one pearl of great price,
> Went and sold all that he had, and bought it.

> *St Matthew 13:45–46*

Here Jesus points out that the pearl of mystic enlightenment
is of such great value that it surpasses that of all other lesser

pearls or goals of this world. The goals, desires and attach-
ments of the world should all be subordinated to this higher
goal.

Again, Jesus says:

> Give not that which is holy unto the dogs,
> Neither cast ye your pearls before swine,
> Lest they trample them under their feet,
> And turn again and rend you.

St Matthew 7:6

Here the pearls refer both to the spiritual teachings and also
to spiritual or mystical experiences. Jesus says never to waste
time trying to convince worldly-minded people of the spiritual
path, and never to disclose inner, spiritual experiences to
others, for they will never appreciate what is being told to
them. They will only "turn again and rend you" – they will
only want to dispute and argue with you and may even harm
you physically or put you to death. At any rate, they are likely
to disturb your peace of mind. Or by sharing your treasures
with those who do not appreciate them, you will feel a loss of
depth in yourself.

Again, in the *Acts of John*, the Word, Logos, or Life Stream
itself is referred to as the "True Pearl Ineffable".

> We glorify Thy Name
>   that was spoken through the Son . . .
>
> We glorify Thy Way; we glorify Thy Seed,
>   the Logos, Grace, Faith, Salt, True Pearl Ineffable,
>   the Treasure, the Plough, the Net,
>   the Greatness, the Diadem,
> Him that for us was called [became] the Son of Man,
>   that gave us Truth, Rest, Knowledge, Power,
>   the Commandment, the Confidence, Hope, Love,
>   Liberty, Refuge in Thee.

For Thou Lord, art alone the root of immortality,
    and the fount of incorruption,
    and the seat of the ages:

Called by all these names for us now,
    that calling on Thee by them
    we may make known [come to know] Thy greatness
    which at the present is invisible to us,
    but visible only to the pure,
    being manifested in thy manhood only.

Acts of John 109, ANT p. 268

And in a similar passage from the *Acts of Peter*, Jesus himself
is described by reference to many of his sayings and parables,
including the pearl and the treasure:

This Jesus ye have, brethren, the Door, the Light,
    the Way, the Bread, the Water, the Life,
    the Resurrection, the Refreshment, the Pearl,
    the Treasure, the Seed, the Abundance [harvest],
    the Mustard Seed, the Vine, the Plough,
    the Grace, the Faith, the Word:
He is all things and there is none other greater than he.

Acts of Peter III:XX, ANT p. 322

And in the *Gospel of Philip*, one of the gnostic treatises
discovered this century in the Egyptian desert, the writer
compares the soul to a pearl which always retains its value
whether it is thrown into the mud, getting covered with the
dirty wrappings of mind and body, or whether it is made to
shine by polishing with balsam oil. To the Father, the soul
always remains his dear and precious son, always retaining its
divine value in His eyes.

When the pearl is cast down into the mud
    it does not lose its value,

Or if it is anointed with balsam oil
  will it become more precious.
But it always has value in the eyes of its owner.

Compare the sons of God, wherever they may be.
They retain their value in the eyes of their Father.

Gospel of Philip 62:17–25, NHL p. 147, GS p. 337

It is very clear, then, that the use of the word "pearl" was full of multiple allusions to the mystic reality. It meant the pearls of wisdom or the true teachings; it referred to the inner experiences of the soul, to the soul itself, or to the soul's knowledge or gnosis of itself; it signified the supreme spiritual goal of meeting and merging with the Lord Himself. It is also symbolic of the Creative Word and, as we shall see, of baptism or initiation into this Word by a "Brother", by a perfect Master.

THE DESCENT OF THE SOUL

I quitted the East [and] went down,
There being with me two guides,
For the way was dangerous and difficult,
And I was young to tread it.

So the soul leaves the "East", its kingly abode with its divine "parents", and because the soul has had no experience of the creation, the way appears dangerous and difficult. Two "guides", says the mystic poet, are therefore required.

The two "guides" are the two primary faculties of the soul – the power to see and the power to hear. This is most important for it is part and parcel of the fact that the Word has two fundamental characteristics – those of Light and of Sound. They are a Divine Light and a Heavenly Sound into which the soul merges itself on its journey homewards.

If we find ourselves in an utterly dark and unfamiliar place, our first instincts are to stand still – and to look and to listen.

Even at this physical level these are primary faculties. Then, if we can hear some sound or see some light, that gives us an indication of where we are. We need a perception of sound and light to get along in this world. Similarly, in all the spheres of creation, the twin faculties of the soul – to see light and to hear sound – are its fundamental attributes.

> I passed the borders of Maishan,
> The meeting place of the merchants of the East,
> And I reached the land of Babel,
> And I entered the walls of Sarbug.
> I went down into Egypt,
> And my guides parted from me.

The poet is describing the descent of the soul to the physical world. Descending from above, Maishan is the last truly spiritual region, lying above the realms of the *greater Mind*. Here meet the "merchants of the East" – the "merchants" of God are the perfect Masters. This phrase is used later, where it will be discussed more fully.

So the soul leaves its home, passes out of the purely spiritual regions and comes to the realm of "Babel". This legendary city, normally presumed to refer to Babylon, is famous from the Jewish book of *Genesis* as the place where Jehovah is said to have poured confusion upon those attempting to build a tower up to God, by making them all speak in different languages.

The true pathway of ascent to God is to travel, mystically, upon His creative outpouring, the Word; and the great and only obstacle standing in the way of the soul is the Mind. Mind is the power which is primarily responsible for the apparent or illusory division of the One Word into the myriad forms and rhythms we experience in the physical creation. It is the creator of the physical, astral and causal domains, and our individual human mind[1] is only one small part of all that goes to make up this greater Mind. The greater Mind is the

---

[1] Where 'mind' refers to the individual, human mind, it is spelt with a small 'm'. Where it refers to the greater Mind, it has been capitalized.

creator of time and space, birth and
inertia, and all the pairs of opposites
familiar – hot and cold, up and down, n
and bad, positive and negative and
Everything that lies within the physi
realms is of the greater Mind. The Mind
and the administrator of these regions, the highest
in these realms of the Mind being termed the Universal
Mind.

And it is this tremendous confusion, diversity and change
within the creation which keeps the soul away from God. The
immense power of the greater Mind is therefore referred
to here as Babel – a truly apt description, for it is Mind
alone which confuses and holds back the soul on its ascent to
God.

From the greater Mind, the soul descends lower to the
region of individual mind – the physical universe – here
symbolized as the "walls of Sarbug". And it is due to the
egocentric confinement exacted by the individual human
mind that the soul falls into Egypt, the physical body, and is
born in this world.

Here, says the poet, the soul's "guides" – its capacity to see
and to hear – part company with it. That is to say, the soul
is so deeply immersed in this world that it is no longer aware
of its innate ability to see and to hear inside – to travel on the
Life Stream and to be conscious of the Light and Sound within
itself. So it can be said to have 'parted company' with these
two faculties or "guides". It has forgotten its origin. It is
certainly true that for the majority of us, when we close our
eyes, we neither see any light nor hear any sound within.

The geography of the soul's journey down to Egypt and its
eventual return is consistent within the poem, and the place
names suggest some interesting allusions. The city of Maishan
lay between Mesopotamia and the sea, a little to the south of
the present-day city of Basra, now in Iraq. The meeting place
of sea-borne commerce from India, in the East, and Babylonia
in the West, Maishan would have been a most significant
point along the trade route, where those arriving from the
West met with their counterparts from the East.

, too, in the soul's descent, "Maishan" – the last of the
ly spiritual regions, unmixed with Mind – is its last true
basis, for after this it is subject to the Mind and its tendencies
and is no longer free. Once a soul is associated with the Mind,
where it goes is then determined by the law of the Mind. The
soul has thus lost its innate freedom. Above the Mind, the soul
is naked and knows itself as pure soul. But once it tastes the
fruit of the Mind, it becomes clothed with separation, division
and duality.

Sarbug is more puzzling, but some help is derived from the
available ancient Greek translations which render it as
"Labyrinth". In the individual human minds are etched the
impressions of the multiplicity of deeds, desires and thoughts
which go to make up a lifetime. Then, after death, and due
entirely to these attractions and uncompleted associations,
the soul is forced to take another birth into the physical arena
which it has so recently vacated. This process goes on for life
after life. The impressions of the past are projected forward
to create the complex patterns of destiny in the next life.
Whatever is not used in the fabrication of one life's destiny is
held within the mind for future use. And this great store-
house of unfulfilled mental entanglements and accretions
increases from life to life. Indian mystics have called it
karma.

After millions upon millions of lifetimes, the unfathomable
complexity of this tapestry can be readily imagined and it is
from this immense mental entanglement that the labyrinth of
the physical realm is being continuously created.

A labyrinth is a place where one gets lost almost imme-
diately. It is even designed for such a purpose. In the physical
universe we are so thoroughly lost, and have been so for such
countless ages, taking birth after birth, that we do not even
realize that we *are* lost. Yet no one knows with certainty what
is going to happen to them in the next two minutes. And
no one can deny that the affairs of the physical universe
constitute so incredibly complex a labyrinth that no human
can even begin to really comprehend it. The word, therefore,
has been well chosen.

It is from Sarbug, then – from the complexities created
and remaining within our individual minds – that the soul

descends into Egypt, the physical body. Our joint minds – only apparently individual and separate, but actually very much a part of the greater Mind – have quite literally become the shareholders and co-creators of our bodies, our destinies and the entire physical universe.

Egypt, of course, is the seat and symbol of ancient exile, captivity and slavery, a metaphor used by many mystic schools of the period in reference to the physical plane in general, as well as to the soul's captivity in a physical body. One could give many examples of this from the ancient literature.

ASLEEP IN EGYPT

> I betook me straight to the serpent,
> Hard by his dwelling I abode,
> [Waiting] till he could slumber and sleep,
> And I could take my pearl from him.

So the soul immediately seeks out the abode of the "serpent" – the lower aspects of the human mind, bedevilled by the emotions and the senses – and watches there until that "loud-breathing" monster begins to sleep and the soul can escape with its pearl, its own innate spiritual wealth.

But the human mind never sleeps – it is always active and busy with its desires and passions in this world. The parents, the Lord, *appear* to have sent the soul upon a hopeless mission. All the same, the parents do know what they are doing.

> And when I was single and alone,
> A stranger to those with whom I dwelt,
> One of my race, a free-born man,
> From among the Easterns, I beheld there –
> A youth fair and well-favoured,
> And he came and attached himself to me.
> And I made him my intimate,
> A comrade with whom I shared my merchandise.

The soul is the real Self. But as the soul descends from God, the Mind takes on the appearance of self, though the sense of self experienced through the mind is actually of an illusory nature. The reality of the soul is that of God – that is, the Source of all. But the mind comes between as an illusory sense of self – a little self, the ego. This separation and beginnings of ego, though still extremely subtle, begins in the realm of the Universal Mind. But by the time the soul has taken on coarser and coarser coverings of the Mind and has taken birth in the physical universe, its complete isolation is effected. It is wearing an impenetrable and hard covering of adamant.

Hence the poet says, "when I was single and alone". Now we are so isolated that we have an individual, human mind which has projected us into an individual physical body. We are so isolated and lost in our small sense of self, our ego, that we have very little idea what other people are thinking or feeling, or why they think and feel like they do. Indeed, we maintain that our own beliefs and way of looking at things are completely true without our ever knowing how or why we actually hold those beliefs or look at things in that way.

We support the reality of our ego, our false identity, at any and all costs without our ever receiving any inkling of the nature of our true Self. We are truly single and alone, bereft of any true soul companions, for we do not even know that our true Self is that of soul, free from all association with the Mind. Indeed, we do not even understand the nature of our body, nor of our mind, let alone of our soul.

Yet – being isolated – the real spiritual seeker feels like a stranger in this world. There is always something within him which tells him that something is missing, that this world is not his real home. So, though he lives here like everyone else, yet he often feels like a stranger and a sleep-walker. Such feelings are a great blessing, for they herald the onset of the great journey homeward.

Feeling in such a way, the soul is naturally attracted to those of a like mind, to fellow seekers, to other souls whose yearnings are for their "Eastern" origin with the Source of Light. So, says Bar Daisan, the soul meets such a person and they become intimate comrades, sharing their "merchandise"

– the spiritual yearnings that they carry with them as their most treasured possessions.

The poet continues:

> And he warned me against the Egyptians
> And against consorting with the unclean;
> For I had put on a garb like theirs,
> Lest they should insult me
> Because I had come from afar,
> To take away the pearl,
> And lest they should arouse the serpent against me.

So the soul is warned by his companion not to consort with the "Egyptians" – the worldly-minded, the unliberated souls who are thoroughly engrossed in the affairs of physical living – for one's mind is affected by the company one keeps, and the subtle, inward atmosphere of spirituality is easily tainted and even lost. Indeed, the soul had already put on a garb like the "Egyptians", so as not to appear different. People of this world are generally upset by those who think or behave in a radically different manner from themselves. Therefore, while it is advisable not to flaunt one's spiritual ideals before all and sundry, the reverse of the coin is that through fear of their critisism and adverse opinion, one copies them, inadvertently becoming like them.

People whose minds are deeply involved in the world and its activities are never sympathetic to those who turn away from the world in search of the spiritual. They oppose those "who are taking away the pearl". Their minds are automatically disturbed by it – "they arouse the serpent" against the soul.

In the story, then, the soul is unable to follow the advice of its noble and intimate comrade. But even though it wears a garment like those of the Egyptians – that is, the soul is incarnate in this world – all the same the Egyptians notice that there is a difference.

> But in some way or other
> They perceived that I was not their countryman.
> And with guile they mingled for me a deceit

And I tasted of their food.
I forgot that I was a son of kings,
And I served their king;
And I forgot the pearl,
For which my parents had sent me,
And by reason of the heaviness of their food,
I fell into a deep sleep.

Although people of the world cannot grasp for certain what it is about mystics and real spiritual seekers that is different, like children who unthinkingly pick upon the odd one out, they sense that there is some essential dissimilarity between them. "They perceive" that the seekers and mystics are "not their countrymen". For this reason, many mystics have even been murdered. This was the fate which befell both Jesus and John the Baptist. In India, too, as well as in Persia, mystics have been tortured and killed. In ancient Greece, Socrates was made to drink a cup of poison for 'perverting' the minds of the young people. Jesus's only 'fault' was that he claimed to have a kingdom. When Pilate asked him where that kingdom was, he replied, "My kingdom is not of this world," adding elsewhere, "The kingdom of God is within you." Yet for this he was crucified, since he appeared to be a threat to the authorities of the time.

People of the world are often disconcerted by mystics. Priests, especially, feel a threat to their power and livelihood, for mystics talk of God with great authority. Yet they adhere to no particular religion. They satisfy the deep spiritual longing within people's hearts. And they take no money or anything else for their personal gain. They are also able to interpret the teachings of past mystics – which often make up the major portion of religious scriptures – in a manner quite different from that of the priests. The Masters teach that God is not to be found in temples, mosques, churches or any man-made building. They point out that He is not to be worshipped by set prayers and rituals. Nor do they want people to believe all manner of strange dogmas in the hope of attaining an unspecified form of salvation. They only advocate seeking Him within oneself, that the relationship of the soul with God is individual and that no priest is required as a mediator. They want each soul to conduct its own independent experiment with Truth.

So, naturally, the priests feel concerned for their livelihood and authority. For this reason, it has frequently been they who have been responsible for the persecution and martyrdom of mystics.

Similarly, materially minded people want those of a mystic inclination to be like them. In fact, it is a common human attribute to want all other people to think and to be like oneself, even though such a thing is obviously impossible, as well as undesirable. Clearly, the world could not function if we were all the same in outward characteristics.

So it is to this sense of difference that our poet is referring. He relates that the "Egyptians" somehow perceived that the soul was not "their countryman" and "with guile they mingled for me a deceit and I tasted of their food". Metaphorically, the "food" of the materially minded is that of worldliness – the busy-ness of a mind deeply attached to and involved with worldly living. It is the food of the passions: lust, anger, greed, attachment and egotism. It is the mind's obsession with the things of the physical senses.

Such food can also be understood literally as the flesh of dead creatures. Mystics of the highest order have always advocated pure vegetarianism for their initiates. Many of the early Christians were also vegetarian, and there are a number of passages in the four canonical gospels and epistles of St Paul, as well as the early apocryphal and gnostic writings, which indicate that Jesus, too, almost certainly taught and practised vegetarianism. Such restrictions to diet and conduct, however, are amongst the first casualties in the process by which a mystic's teachings become a religion, and later interpolations, interpretations, mistranslations and general editorial tampering by interested parties have greatly confused the matter.

Vegetarianism is considered essential because impressions are left upon the mind which relate to all an individual's deeds, desires and attachments in this world. And killing for one's food leaves a considerable residue upon the mind, because of involvement in the suffering caused to such unlucky creatures.

These impressions remain, to be paid off in future lives, and
thus a diet of animals, birds, fish and indeed anything outside
the plant kingdom is a great hindrance to spiritual progress.
The eating of one's fellow creatures is a major factor amongst
the processes which keep souls within the regions of Mind and
the turbulent sea of physical death and rebirth.

Real spiritual progress takes place as the mental accretions
from a myriad past lives are slowly erased. So if we are
continually accumulating mental impressions, whilst at the
same time attempting to erase them – then spiritual progress
is impaired. We must also respect the life in other creatures if
we wish to increase the stature of our own inner life.

So, by eating the "food" of the Egyptians, by entanglement
in the realm of physical incarnation, the soul becomes full of
worldliness and moves in the ways of the worldly mind. With
the result, says the poet, that:

> I forgot that I was a son of kings,
> Anc I served their king;
> And I forgot the pearl,
> For which my parents had sent me,
> And by reason of the heaviness of their food,
> I fell into a deep sleep.

The incessant activity of the mind makes the soul forget its
divine nature. It forgets that it is a "son of kings" – a son of
God. Instead, it serves the king of the Egyptians, the Mind.

It is this king or ruler, also known as the Universal Mind
or the Negative Power, that Jesus and other mystics of his era
called Satan, Belial, Beelzebub, the Devil, the Wicked One,
the Sinner, the Enemy, the Adversary, the Prince of the
World, the Prince of Darkness, the Demiurge, Ialdabaoth,
Babel and by many other names. For the individual mind is
the agent of this Universal Mind and the royal soul goes
wherever the wilful mind takes it. The soul can thus be said
to serve the king, not only of this world, but of all the three
worlds of the Mind. Then the soul becomes a servant of the
Devil and, as a consequence, it forgets the pearl – the spiritual
purpose of life, for which the Lord has sent us here and given
us a human body. In fact, this food of the world lies so heavily

upon the mind that the soul falls to lower and lower states of consciousness. So unconscious do we become that we are effectively fast asleep. We are awake to the world, no doubt. But we are fast asleep as far as the true nature of our soul, our innermost Self, is concerned. So it is well said that the soul has fallen fast asleep.

Many mystics have also described the state of the soul in this world as being dead. The soul, caught in the grip of the mind, constantly enters and re-enters the arena where death is the only certain reality. Consequently, this world is described as the region of death and darkness, as opposed to God who is the source of real life and light. There are many references to this in the Christian gospels and in the writings of other mystics.

In St John's gospel, for example, Jesus says to his disciples:

> I am the light of the world,
> He that followeth me shall not walk in darkness,
> But shall have the light of life.
>
> *St John 8:12*

And again:

> Whosoever liveth
> And believeth in me
> Shall never die.
>
> *St John 11:26*

And:

> The dead shall hear the Voice
> Of the Son of God:
> And they that hear shall live.
>
> *St John 5:25*

Or in the deeply devotional and mystic *Odes of Solomon*, written in early Christian times, the poet – writing in the

name of the Master (though who he was is not mentioned)
– says:

> Death disgorged me and many with me: . . .
> And I made an assembly of living men
>   among his dead.
> And I spoke to them with living lips,
> In order that my Word might not be without effect.
> And those who had died ran to me,
> And cried and said,
> "Have pity on us, Son of God! . . .
> And bring us out of the bonds of darkness.
> And open for us the gate.
> That by it, we may come out with thee,
> For we see that death does not touch thee,
> Because thou art our deliverer."
>
> *Odes of Solomon XLII, AOT p. 731*

And in the Manichaean writings, we find:

> Abandon sleep, awake, behold the light
> Which is drawn near.
> He has come to the world!
> All the sons of Darkness hide.
> The Light is come, and near [is] the dawn!
> Arise brethren, give praise!
> We shall forget the dark night.
>
> *MMP pp. 50–51*

These passages all have the same meaning – that a perfect,
living mystic is an incarnation or embodiment of the Word.
He is the source of life and light for his disciples. But he must
be living. He must speak "with living lips" to ensure that his
"Word might not be without effect". "Whosoever *liveth*" is
also emphasized in St John's gospel. A living human being has
to meet a living Master.

So the mystic takes birth in the realm where the light is
extinguished and life is encompassed by death. And by means

of the Word, the Voice of the Son of God, he awakens the sleeping souls, he raises them from the dead.

He makes them see the light of life within themselves. He gathers together "an assembly of living men among the dead", taking them out of the realm of death, darkness and slumber so that they may live forever with the Lord and never die again.

All this, our poet will describe.

THE COMING OF THE WORD – THE ADVENT OF THE MASTER

The poem continues:

> But all those things that befell me,
> My parents perceived and were grieved for me.

The poet says that the Lord never ceased caring for the soul which He had sent into the creation and who had forgotten its purpose in being there. The Lord never forgets His purpose. Everything happens as He wills, in His own good time.

> And a proclamation was made in our kingdom,
> That all should speed to our gate,
> Kings and princes of Parthia
> And all the great ones of the East.
> So they wove a plan on my behalf,
> That I might not be left in Egypt.

The Lord does not prevent the soul from falling into this deep sleep. After all, He is the one who has created such a creation. It is a part of His plan that the soul should be caught under the spell of the mind. But the time comes when He wishes to remedy the situation, to fulfil His greater purpose. So the "kings and princes" are summoned to the aid of the soul. Such kings and princes are the perfect Masters. They are the "great ones of the East", the ones who come from the source of light

and life, sent by the Lord to collect the souls He has marked
for them and to take them back to God.

> And they wrote to me a letter,
> And every noble signed his name thereto.

The succinct mystical metaphors of these two lines point, in
a hidden way, to the practice of meditation given by all perfect
Masters to their disciples. First of all, the "letter" is the
Creative Word of God – the creative power which underlies
and energizes the whole creation and which lies within us. It
is one with God and one with our own soul. When the correct
technique is practised, this Word, like a letter, can be *heard*
in mystic transport, within ourselves. It is not heard in earthly
words but as a divine and rapturous music. This is the true
"music of the spheres", as the Greek mystics called it. And,
like a letter, this Word also conveys a special message and
call – beckoning the earthbound soul homewards. A letter,
too, is always borne by a messenger. In this case, the
Messenger of the "parents" letter is a perfect Master.

A true Master first of all re-tunes the soul of his disciple to
this inner creative power. This piece of mystic 'engineering' is
what constitutes the real initiation or baptism with the Word
of God. The Master himself is the Word incarnate. He is the
"Word made flesh", as it says in St John's gospel. The Master
is the realized Son of God, born of the pure Virgin Light.
The Word itself is "only-begotten" (from the Greek, *mono-
genes*, meaning – more correctly – 'alone-begotten' or 'self-
begotten'), signifying that the Creative Word is the primary
emanation or 'Son' of God the Father. No other power is
involved in the emanation of the Word, for there is none
other. But this does not mean that the human body of a
Master is born in a miraculous manner, without a father or
a mother. Nor does it mean that there is only one physical
Master for all times and all peoples.

The physical form of a Master is not the real Master, any
more than our physical body constitutes our real Self. The real
Master is the Word itself which is in that body and which
gives it life.

Listening to this Divine Music or Creative Word is the

technique which takes a soul back to God. And for this the baptism and personal guidance of a perfect Master is required. No one else can give this initiation or baptism on his behalf. Nor is it the right of any soul to receive such a baptism merely by asking. A Master is appointed by God and possesses the power and the right to give the initiation only to those who have been marked or sealed for him, by the Father, by God.

Each Master comes for his own appointed lost sheep, his marked sheep – not for any others. And each marked soul must be initiated while the Master is still living in the body. A Master who has left his body cannot give initiation to souls still living in this world any more than a dead doctor can treat a living patient. For souls who are to be initiated today, there will be another Master – a living Master. In fact, it is a built-in part of the creation that there is *always* at least one perfect Master alive on the earth. There can even be more than one Master alive at the same time.

So for the king and princes to write a letter to the soul means that the soul receives the message of the Word, is initiated or baptized by a living Master of the Word.

Then the mystic poet adds, "And every noble signed his name thereto." This also contains a deep mystical meaning. Each region of the Lord's creation is, so to say, 'ruled' by a power, by a 'substation' of the Word. The Universal Mind or Satan, for example, is such a power, known to the gnostics and other mystics by many names. This power, taking its own power and authority from the Supreme Being, through the Word, creates and administers all of the lower creation – the three worlds of the Mind.

The rulers of the inner mansions of creation are referred to here as the "nobles" who sign their name to the mystic letter. This refers to two aspects of the instruction given by a perfect Master. Firstly, as we have already mentioned in passing, the Creative Word of God is frequently spoken of by mystics as His *Name*. When God is one, then there is no room for names. When there is no division, when all is one, who is to call another by name? When God projects His Word, it can be said that this constitutes the first division or emanation of Himself. Now there are two, (though the two are one!).

Therefore, this emanation is known as God's Name.

The Name or Word of God can be heard within, in meditation. The Word is the dynamic power of God, manifesting the many levels of creation. As the soul ascends on this current during meditation, it seems to sound differently at each level. Each ruler can therefore be said to possess his own individual 'name' or distinctive sound. This is the inner, esoteric, unspoken and utterly non-physical name of each ruler. Therefore, the poet says that each "noble" or ruler "signs" his name to the letter – the Word. A signature is individually recognizable, just as the music of the Word appears to possess a uniquely distinctive sound in each region.

To make it understandable at our physical level – the level of words and physical noises – mystics have given each of these rulers some verbal name or other so as to differentiate them and give us some limited idea of the extent and arrangement of the inner creation. Different mystics have given them different names in different languages.

And these spoken names also have another purpose. The Masters are aware that although the Word is resounding within every soul, initiated or not, we do not actually hear it. The reason for this is the "loud-breathing serpent" – the passions, emotions and desires – the lower aspects of the human mind. The attention of the mind is so completely drawn out into the world by the senses and emotions, it is caught up so much with the activities and busy-ness of living here, that it does not even suspect the existence of the inner sound, let alone listen for it.

Our minds are constantly busy with thoughts concerning the physical world. These thoughts then lead to actions or remain as unfulfilled desires. Either way, they make continual impressions upon the mind, and the attention remains locked on to the things and ideas of the world. This is the "deceit" of the world and the "heaviness of its food". And the soul thus remains "fast asleep in Egypt".

For the soul to awaken, this mental worldliness needs to be stilled. And to understand how this is to be accomplished, the situation needs to be studied in a little greater detail. Mystics teach that the seat of the soul and mind in the physical body is located in the forehead, behind and slightly above the two physical eyes. This point has been called the eye centre or third eye. Jesus refers to it as the single eye when he says:

> The light of the body is the eye:
> If, therefore, thine eye be single,
> Thy whole body shall be full of light.
>
> But if thine eye be evil,
> Thy whole body shall be full of darkness.
> If therefore the light that is in thee be darkness,
> How great is that darkness!
>
> *St Matthew 6:22–23*

It is from this eye centre or single eye that the soul and mind have spread throughout the body and into the entire world. Additionally, the Divine Music of the Word does not descend below the single eye. An individual, therefore, whose mind and soul are scattered away from this centre can neither hear the Word, nor be in a position to be pulled up by it. The first part of the meditational practice is therefore to withdraw the mind and soul from both the body and the world and to concentrate and still it at this centre, from where it can catch the Music of the Word.

Observing, however, that we are in the habit of continuously thinking, mystics know that there is no point in simply telling us to stop thinking, for we cannot do so. It is not that simple. They therefore tell us to *mentally* repeat certain words or names – which they give to us – with the attention fixed at the single eye. This method helps to concentrate the mind. And the names which they give are the names of the rulers or "nobles" of the inner regions.

These names, or holy names, are the carrier wave, so to speak, of the divine power. The names themselves, being associated in our minds only with the inner journey, also direct the consciousness inwards and upwards. The human mind works by habit and association. Therefore, if mystics were to tell us to repeat the names of any objects or actions in *this* world, we would immediately begin thinking about the world and would remain in the world.

It is by repetition of the thoughts of the world that the mind runs out. Then, at death, since the mind has been so fascinated with the world, the soul, captivated by its association with the mind, immediately takes another birth here in order to fulfil all those desires and reap the fruit of its previous actions. But by repetition of the names of the "nobles", the mind begins to concentrate and, by degrees, under the guidance of a Master, it comes into contact with the inner music of the Word. Every "noble" can thus be said to have "signed his name" to our release.

These two seemingly innocent lines of narrative, therefore, contain a wealth of mystic meaning.

THE CALL OF THE MASTER

There is, then, great significance to the mystic "letter," sent by the king to the lost soul, and signed by each of his nobles. And what is it that the letter 'says'? The poet writes:

> "From thy Father, the King of kings,
> And thy Mother, the Mistress of the East,
> And from thy Brother, our next in rank,
> To thee our son, who art in Egypt, greeting!
> Up and arise from thy sleep,
> And listen to the words of our letter!
> Call to mind that thou art a son of kings!
> See the slavery – [and] whom thou servest!
> Remember the pearl
> For which thou didst speed to Egypt!
> Think of thy bright robe,
> And remember thy glorious toga,
> Which thou shalt put on as thine adornment.
> Thy name is named in the book of life,
> And with thy Brother, whom thou hast received,
> Thou shalt be in [shalt return to] our kingdom."

The "letter" comes from the trinity – the Supreme Lord ("thy Father, the King of kings"), the Word ("thy Mother, the Mistress of the East" – the 'consort' of the Lord), and the perfect Master ("thy Brother, our next in rank.")

The Word is sent as a greeting to the son or soul lost in Egypt or imprisoned in the body. And one can imagine that this greeting of the Lord is no ordinary "Hello!" but a message truly worthy of the Source to a rivulet.

The 'greeting' of the Word calls the soul to awaken from its deep slumber of worldliness and involvement with the mind and to *listen* to the words of the letter. This is a clear reference to listening to the inner sound of the Word, the Sound Current.

"Remember who and what you are," says this mystic call, "a son of kings, a son of God, a drop of His Ocean. Awake and observe your condition of slavery to the mind and the senses – see what it is to which you have become enslaved." "Whom thou servest" therefore refers to Satan, the Universal Mind, the power which rules the three worlds of the Mind.

This power or Satan rules by the law of justice. This is the law of the Mind. "Whatsoever a man soweth, that shall he also reap," as St Paul wrote (*Galatians 6:7*). The law of the Mind, also called the law of *karma*, is cause and effect. It holds sway throughout the three worlds of the Mind. Whatever impressions are formed upon the mind at one time will automatically bear fruit in a corresponding fashion, at some later time – usually in a future life. Whatever may be one's present entanglements, they are not only the result of past associations, but also the seeds for future ensnarement. So those who follow the tendencies of the mind are automatically enslaved by the lord of the Mind – Satan, the Devil, the Negative Power, the Universal Mind. They serve Satan, the Prince of this world.

This "letter" of our poet can be interpreted in both an esoteric and an exoteric manner. On the one hand, it is the Word within that really awakens the soul. This is entirely esoteric, mystical and hidden from our physical eyes and ears. But for this mystical process to reach its final fulfilment, the soul must actually meet a living Master, outside, in the world. And the essence of a mystic's teachings is that the soul is the child of the Lord but has fallen into the clutches of the mind and the senses and needs to be awakened by means of the Word. But this only happens when we come into contact with a fully realized Son of God, a Word made flesh, a perfect Master actually living in the world with us.

A Master tells us about God, about the Word, and about the role of a Master. He teaches the necessity of inner baptism or initiation by the Word. He tells us who we really are and how to regain knowledge, experience or gnosis of that state of consciousness.

Yet though the Master gives his teachings to all who come to him, only those whose "name is named in the book of life" will actually find themselves interested in what he has to say. These are the sheep who are marked for that Master to initiate and to take back to the Lord. To begin with, when the time is right for a marked soul to receive initiation, it feels that its interest in the spiritual teachings of a Master is of its own creation. But in fact it is the Word or Master within who is pulling the strings, and generating that interest in the soul. The pull actually comes from within. It is the mystic Word within, which is really at work. The outer, physical form of the Master is only a personification of that Word, a necessary focus for the senses, intelligence and love of the seeker – necessary because in our present state of spiritual blindness and deafness we are unable to contact the Word in its pure state.

So the Master says to each marked soul, "Remember the pearl for which thou didst speed to Egypt." And because the power of the Word is at work inside, the soul understands and agrees with what the Master is saying outwardly. The letter, therefore, also refers to the outer teaching of the Master, as well as to the inner pull of the Word. All the Masters remind us to remember the true purpose of life.

"Think of thy bright robe and remember thy glorious toga, which thou shalt put on as thine adornment." The Master reminds us of the beauty and glory of our true home, its happiness, bliss, love and light.

Then the letter says, "Thy name is named in the book of life," indicating to the soul that it has been marked or allotted "to thy Brother" – the soul's appointed Master – "to be in our kingdom" – to return to God. In other gnostic writings of this period, God is also called Great Life. For God is the Ocean of Life, Consciousness or Being. Hence He is also called the Supreme Being.

This does not mean that a soul who is called by the Master experiences no struggles thereafter. Quite the reverse, in fact. For now the old tendencies of the mind towards self-centred, outward living are challenged by the inward pull of the Master. The resulting struggle – being filled with doubts one day and faith the next, full of love today and dryness tomorrow, the disinclination towards the world of the senses and yet its inexorable drawing power, one's attempts to become detached in the midst of attachment – this struggle continues until one begins to concentrate at the single eye and gain some small degree of control, however fluctuating, over the mind.

Continuing, the poet says,

> And my letter [was] a letter
> Which the King [as ambassador
> Had] sealed with his right hand,
> To keep it from the wicked ones,
> The children of Babel,
> And from the tyrannous demons of Sarbug.

Mystics always say that the initiate should follow the sound and the light on the right hand path, for this alone leads back to God. Mystic literature of the past, as well as more recent times, has always spoken of the right and left hand paths. Generally, the right hand path is that of pure spirituality, leading to the highest mystic attainment, while the left hand path refers to the paths of magic, psychism, spirit contact and so on.

Just as we divide life into good and bad or right and wrong, so too do we talk of right and left in mysticism. Those paths or practices which stimulate the mind and keep one bound to the mind constitute the "left hand path". Their tendency is to keep the soul captive within the worlds of the Mind, especially this world.

The right hand path, on the other hand, is the path that

leads the soul out of the realms of the Mind and back to God. And this means to be in mystic contact with the Word – the Divine Music and Divine Light, the path or current which ascends to God.

So firstly, the Master, the ambassador of God, is sealed by God. He is appointed to do his work of ferrying souls across the creation, back to the Lord. Secondly, the Master must be a Master of the right hand path.

There are many mystics who come to this world from other parts of the Lord's creation, usually from within the Mind regions. These are the "children of Babel". Their mission, though essential, is mostly that of mystic social workers, keeping the creation in a tolerable condition.

Their teachings will usually reflect this purpose. Mostly, they do not claim to take souls out of the realm of birth and death because they themselves do not know the way. Often, they only teach peace in this world and not how to escape from it permanently. They may not teach any meditation at all. Or they may teach only a very simple and popular form, to be practised only for short periods of time. They do not teach the secret of contacting the Word and meditation upon its Divine Music as the only means of salvation from death and rebirth.

Furthermore, since they too are within the realms of the Mind, they come here according to their own past history of lives. They are not themselves free souls. Therefore, unlike perfect Masters, they cannot be true givers, for they have not the power to organize their own lives or destinies. For this reason, they will often need to *ask* their disciples for money or subsistence – either for themselves or for their organization.

A true Master, on the other hand, has his life and destiny entirely under his control and he is always the giver. He is one with the Lord himself and nothing can ever be given to the One who is already within everything. Everything already belongs to the Lord, it is a part of Him. But only a perfect Master is in such a unique position. All other souls are within the realm of giving and taking, and are constrained to act accordingly. And "if the blind lead the blind, both shall fall into the ditch" (*St Matthew 15:14*).

The physically incarnate individual, therefore, being quite blind to the inner attainment of any other souls in this world, is entirely dependent upon the grace and blessings of the Lord in finding a perfect Master. A blind man cannot catch hold of one with eyes. He has to wait until the hand of compassion reaches out to him. But, by divine and mystic design, the deep and sincere desire to find God will only arise in those souls who are destined, sooner or later, to find a perfect Master. No one need fear disappointment. The seeking and the finding are perfectly matched partners, in all spheres of life. But in the meantime, and in this apparent search, one should use the very best of one's discrimination in deciding who really is a perfect Master and only make a choice when the pull from within and one's own personal conviction are too strong to resist.

Like naive, modern religious concepts of Satan, the word 'demon', or more correctly 'daemon', had a different meaning in our poet's era. Even Plato wrote, "All that lies between God and Man is daemonian." The demons were (and are) a general name for any powers in the hierarchy of creation, like the 'nobles' or rulers of the regions. In particular, they are powers within the Mind worlds. Different writers of antiquity have used the term in different ways, but demons also refer to the powers and passions to be found within our human mind. Thus the "tyrannous demons of Sarbug" and the "loud-breathing serpent" are of similar ilk.

All the powers of the Mind keep the soul within the realms of the Mind, under the law of the Mind. They are thus tyrants, for the soul is not free. It is completely imprisoned by the Mind. And all these powers can be called "demons". The human passions and the forces of destiny are like iron chains, keeping the soul forcibly bound to the physical world, while the mystical powers and lesser mystics who come from within the Mind regions are like golden chains, keeping us happily bound – but prisoners, nonetheless. But both are "daemonian" – of the Mind.

In fact, Satan, the Universal Mind, was also known to the gnostics as the 'Demiurge', to which the "demons" were related as sub-powers. So when it describes in the gospels how the Master Jesus "cast out demons", this is exactly true.

All Masters help their disciples to become free from the
dominion of the mind, to "cast out their demons". But these
are not demons with red hairy faces, pointed ears and forked
tails!

INITIATION OR BAPTISM

Then, again describing the characteristics of this mystic letter,
the poet continues:

> It flew in the likeness of an eagle,
> The king of all the birds;
> It flew and alighted beside me,
> And became all-speech.

These lines are immediately reminiscent of the baptism of
Jesus, where the Word or Holy Ghost was said to have
descended like a dove. This, of course, has been externalized
as a physical event by those who did not understand the
spiritual reality of true initiation. Initiation, however, has
been likened to the descent of a bird in a number of the gnostic
writings of this period. The bird, like the Word, comes from
on high and alights beside us. It then flies away, high into the
sky. Similarly, the Word comes from the highest level of Spirit
within, and taking birth in this world alights at our level as a
perfect Master. The Master alights beside the incarnate soul.
He brings the Word with him, so to speak, and initiates or
baptizes the soul.

So again, the poetry has a double meaning, inner and
outer – the descent of the Word in initiation and the descent
of the Word as a physically incarnate, perfect Master, who
can walk and talk and laugh with us at our level. But the two
meanings are part and parcel of the same greater reality – that
of the salvation of the soul by the great creative power of God,
the Word, and its personification, the Master.

At the time of initiation, the Master also alights within the
mind of the disciple, just as a dove was said to alight –
symbolically – upon the head of Jesus at the time of his
initiation by John the Baptist. What these lines do not mean

is that a real eagle came and alighted on the ground, any more than in the gospel account it means that a real dove came and sat upon the head of Jesus!

The initiation of a perfect Master is a touch of soul to soul – the soul of the Master to the soul of the disciple. Although practical instructions for meditation are given at this time, no ceremony is involved and the real initiation takes place inside – beyond the ken of the disciple. Like a radio that is switched on but emits no sound, the soul needs to be re-tuned, so to speak, so that the signal which has been there all along can be received or appreciated for what it is.

Then, says the poet (in our English translation), the letter "became all-speech". Again, it seems to mean that the perfect Master speaks or brings the true and correct *spoken* teachings regarding the return of a soul to the Lord. And it also refers to the Word, which is the All-Sound, the all-pervading *unspoken* Sound or Vibration of Life, which is present everywhere and within everything.

THE AWAKENING OF THE SOUL

> At its voice and the sound of its rustling,
> I started and arose from my sleep.
> I took it up and kissed it,
> And loosed its seal, [and] read;
> And according to what was traced on my heart
> Were the words of my letter written.

Here, the poet continues with his double meaning of the outward, physical form of the Master and the inner Word. The soul is awakened by listening inwardly to the music of the Word, the Voice of God. The soul is also awakened by the physical presence and teachings of the Master. Masters have a most beautiful and expressive manner of talking. Their words reach into the hearts of their listeners and ring a thousand bells of truth and beauty.

Inwardly, the soul embraces the Word, becomes very intimate with the Word, "kissing it", expressing its deep love. This is possible because the real essence of the soul *is* this very Word, and its relationship is that of loving and merging.

So the soul "loosed its seal" means that it gradually gained inner access to the Word. And, most beautifully, it found in that experience, its heart's desire – it found that what was written in the letter exactly matched the longing of its inner being, the 'heart' of a soul. The seeking matched the finding. "Seek and ye shall find." What was written in the letter matched the "compact" his parents had earlier written in his heart, so that it should not be forgotten.

It means that the innermost longings of the soul were fully satisfied by absorption in the Divine Music. It also means that the words of the Master satisfied the mind in a manner which is most uncommon. One would never have thought that simple words could be made to convey so much wisdom. The Master's words come with a vibration and a power which penetrate the minds of the listeners, depending upon their receptivity, creating in their wake feelings of intense bliss, happiness and understanding. This process continues for as long as one listens to him. Even the same words, heard over and over again, year after year, still possess a freshness and a sense of revelation which is hard to describe.

Then, through the words of the Master from without and the advent of the Word within:

> I remembered that I was a son of kings,
> And my free soul longed for its natural state.
> I remembered the pearl,
> For which I had been sent to Egypt.

So the soul is awakened and longs to be a free and natural soul, unencumbered by the trappings of mind, body and illusion. It remembers the purpose of its being sent to Egypt, of its being in this physical domain: to rediscover the lost Word within itself.

> And I began to charm him,
> The terrible loud-breathing serpent.
> I hushed him to sleep and lulled him to slumber

By naming the name of my Father upon him,
And the name of our next in rank
And of my Mother, the Queen of the East;
And I snatched away the pearl,
And turned to go back to my Father's house.

So the soul begins to awaken. It charms, hushes to sleep or lulls to slumber the lower mind, the "terrible loud-breathing serpent". This means that the individual begins to meditate – to "charm" the lower mind, to put the mind out of action, to still the mind. And the technique used is "by naming the name of my Father" – to listen to the Name of God, the Word, the soul's Mother, "the Queen of the East". And this mystic Name is also the 'name' of the Master, the "next in rank".

The real Master, the realized Son of God, is one with the Word. This Word is also one with God. Yet this mystery cannot be understood intellectually. Words are only a description of a mystic reality or experience. But it is these three – Father, Son and Holy Ghost (or Word) – which constitute the Christian trinity. Christian theologians have given great thought to the nature of these three. Their earliest traditions clearly indicated their importance. But no theological discussion, intellectual formula or blind belief will ever reveal their mystery.

"Charming" the mind also refers to the first part of the meditational practice: the mental repetition of the "names" of the "nobles" with the attention concentrated at the single eye. This is a "charm" which really works!

And once the mind is "charmed", then the soul "snatches away the pearl" – sets its sights upon spiritual enlightenment or God-realization and starts out upon the royal road, the way back to its divine home, "my Father's house".

THE INNER JOURNEY: ESCAPE FROM EGYPT

Now the mystic poet describes in full the inner journey.

> And their filthy and unclean garb
> I stripped off, and left it in their country,
> And I took my way straight, to come
> To the Light of our home, the East.

The soul and mind withdraw from the body, "the filthy and unclean garb", leaving it in this world, "their country", during meditation. All the concentration of the mind has been focused at the single eye and the soul sets out upon the inner journey, the straight way to God – "the Light of our home, the East".

This is also the true resurrection. The baptized or initiated soul arises from the tomb of the body, from the realm of death, and is led towards the Lord, the ocean and source of life. From death, the soul is resurrected and returned to life. The soul is taught the art of dying while living, of passing through the experience of death while still living in a physical body.

Many of the more mystically inclined among the early Christians fully understood this. In the *Gospel of Philip*, the gnostic writer says:

> Those who say they will die first
>   and then rise are in error.
> If they do not first receive
>   the resurrection while they live,
> When they die they will receive nothing.
>
> *Gospel of Philip 73:1–4, NHL p. 153*

And again:

> It is necessary to rise [whilst living] 'in this flesh',
>   since everything exists [with]in it!
>
> *Gospel of Philip 57:18–19, NHL p. 144*

In other words, everything – God and His entire creation – lie within the body. It is within ourselves that He must be found. But the journey must be begun – can even be completed – whilst still living in the human form. Whatever is to be done should be done now – not left hopefully until after death or for some far off and ill-defined 'day of judgement'. For if the matter is not taken in hand while living, if the orientation of the mind is not directed towards the Lord whilst still in this world, how can it be expected to suddenly change its tendencies after death? The soul goes "where your treasure is" – where the inclinations of the mind take it.

Similarly, in St John's gospel, we find:

> I am the resurrection and the life:
> He that believeth in me, though he were dead,
> Yet shall he live.

St John, 11:25

That is, for his initiates, Jesus is the 'resurrection', the giver of inner life. Those who are dead, those who are living in the grave of the body, they can rise up and find the source of life eternal. Then they can be said to be truly living.

And again:

> The dead shall hear the voice of the Son of God:
> And they that hear shall live. . . .
> All that are in the graves shall hear his voice.

St John 5:25, 28

Here, as in the poem, it is the Voice of the Son, the Music of the Divine Word, which draws the souls out of the grave of the physical body.

THE INNER JOURNEY:
THE LIGHT FORM OF THE MASTER

Then, at the commencement of this journey, the most wonderful event takes place.

> And my letter, my awakener,
> I found before me on the road,
> And as with its voice it had awakened me,

[So] too with its light it was leading me,
Shining before me in a garment of radiance,
Glistening like royal silk.
And with its voice and its guidance,
It also encouraged me to speed,
And with his love was drawing me on.

An individual, at the human level, consists of soul, mind and body. While it is relatively easy to realize that one's true self is not the body, the soul and mind are so helplessly knotted together that it is almost impossible for us to distinguish the one from the other. Our human sense of self therefore consists of a fusion of these two. This can be called the 'individual'. Sometimes one speaks of the soul, but in the Mind regions this always means the soul and mind in combination.

The soul and mind, then, when simplified, purified and concentrated enough to leave the body, pass through the door of brightness, the single eye, and there upon the threshold of the astral realms, the individual meets with the radiant, astral or light form of the Master. Just as in this physical region the Word takes form as the physical body of the Master, so too in the higher regions does the Word take on an appropriate and recognizable form. The Master is the Word personified. His real form is that of the Word. But to whatever level the disciple reaches, there the Master takes on a corresponding form.

The astral form of the Master shines with a deep radiance, scintillating as if sprinkled with star dust, permeating the environment with an atmosphere of great bliss and love. The translators of the poem, at this point, all admit their perplexity. Both James and Wright indicate that a reference is made to "a shining and royal garment of silk" in which the letter is wrapped, while Bevan omits the line altogether. Wright also suggests that the meaning refers to "the dweller in silk".

The rendering suggested, therefore, ("Shining before me in a garment of radiance, glistening like royal silk"), incorporates these images for – mystically speaking – the intended meaning seems clear enough. The radiantly beautiful, astral form of the Master is the "dweller in silk". The real Master is the Word – the "letter" – and the astral form is a royal wrapping for the royal Word, sparkling like silk, shedding light all around. The imagery is both exact and beautiful.

And this light form 'talks' to and communicates with the soul. All its questions are answered. All possible guidance is given to that soul. In this world, many questions have no answers. Words are quite insufficient to describe the inner realities. But there, the awakener is ever present to guide. So, listening to the "voice of the letter", (listening to the melody of the Word), contemplating upon the light form of the Master, and receiving guidance at all times, the soul is continuously encouraged to speed onwards. "And with his love was drawing me on" – the Master showers his incomparable love and blessings upon the soul and, moving inwards and upwards, the enraptured soul follows.

It is due to human limitations that the Word needs to take form in this world as a physical Master. For then he can talk to the souls here and communicate with them in human ways. This is required in order for his disciples to acquire faith and to thoroughly understand his teachings. But human communication has its limitations! In addition, the physical Master cannot always be with all his disciples. He cannot converse with everyone all the time. And one day, like everyone else, he will also leave this world, physically.

But inside, the Master is available to every initiate all the time, even after his departure from this world, if the disciple can reach that point in his meditation. The Word is within everyone, and that Word takes form inside, for every disciple. Then there is no separation, no parting. Then the soul is with the Master forever.

The light form of the Master thus constitutes the 'second coming' of the Master, as described by the Master Jesus in the fourteenth chapter of St John's gospel:

In my Father's house there are many mansions:
If it were not so, I would have told you.
I go to prepare a place for you.
And if I go and prepare a place for you,
I will come again, and receive you unto myself;
That where I am, there ye may be also.

And whither I go, ye know,
And the way ye know. . . .

And I will pray the Father,
And He shall give you another Comforter,
That He may abide with you forever;
Even the Spirit of Truth;
Whom the world cannot receive,
Because it seeth Him not, neither knoweth Him:
But ye know Him; for He dwelleth with[in] you,
And shall be in you.

I will not leave you comfortless: I will come to you.
Yet a little while, and the world seeth me no more;
But ye see me: because I live, ye shall live also.
At that day ye shall know that I am in my Father,
And ye in me, and I in you.

He that hath my commandments and keepeth them,
He it is that loveth me:
And he that loveth me shall be loved of my Father,
And I will love him,
And will manifest myself unto him. . . .

These things have I spoken unto you,
Being yet present with you.
But the Comforter, which is the Holy Ghost,
Whom the Father will send in my name,
He shall teach you all things,
And bring all things to your remembrance,
Whatsoever I have said unto you.

St John 14:2–4, 16–20, 25–26

These poignant words are mirrored in the meaning of our
poem. Though this is not the place for a line-by-line com-
mentary of St John, it is clear from the context that Jesus – in
his human form – is about to leave his disciples and is
comforting them. He will always be with them, he says. "I will
not leave you comfortless. I will come to you." The

Comforter, the Holy Ghost, the radiant or light form of the Master – the "letter" or "awakener" of our poem – is always within a disciple, ready to instruct and guide, "to teach all things." As Jesus says, to *bring all things to your remembrance.*" And this is no ordinary guidance of this world, but a remembrance concerning the knowledge and experience of God, that the soul knew long ago, when it was a little child in its Father's kingdom.

And note, too, that Jesus specifically mentions the "mansions in my Lord's house" in the same context as "going to prepare a place for you", "I will come to you", "sending you the Comforter", and "I will manifest myself to him." This chapter of St John is redolent with deep mystical meaning. That 'coming to you' or 'manifesting' is clearly *within* the disciple and is associated with a meeting in the inner mansions. It is not an outward coming to this world. The 'first coming' is the meeting of the soul with a living Master. The 'second coming' is when the soul meets the light form of the Master within. As the poet says, it shone "before me in a garment of radiance" and "with its light it was leading me on." And that form gives constant "guidance", "encouragement" and "love". This all happens *within* the disciple.

But for that inner meeting to take place each soul must first meet its own personal living Master, in the body. Lasting conviction and real progress only come by personal contact and individual instruction. And in the presence of a Master, a soul is bathed in his blissful atmosphere of sublime spirituality. The experience of spirituality is infused into a person, melting the heart and transmitting a deep mystical understanding.

How many people must have thought, "How lucky were those souls who actually met Jesus!" Yet, against all expectations, against all the odds, this wish can be fulfilled. It is a law of nature. And that meeting is a million times better than one could ever imagine.

So the soul leaves the body and on the way, "on the road", it immediately meets with the light form of the Master who instructs, guides, comforts, loves and draws the soul further onwards.

THE INNER JOURNEY:
THROUGH THE INNER MANSIONS

> I went forth, passed by Sarbug,
> I left Babel on my left hand,
> And reached Maishan the great,
> The haven of the merchants,
> That sitteth on the shore of the sea.

"I went forth" – the soul leaves the body – and "passed by Sarbug" – it goes past the region of the individual human mind, the 'sky' of the body from where the web of destiny is spun. "I left Babel on my left hand" – it travels past the regions of "Babel", the greater Mind. And note that the point is again made that these regions of creation are on the "left hand" side and are to be avoided as distractions from the royal road homewards, following the Word or life stream to its source.

Above the Mind realms, above Babel, the soul reaches "Maishan the great, the haven of the merchants that sitteth on the shore of the sea." As in the earlier description of the soul's descent, Maishan is the first purely spiritual region, unmixed with Mind or matter. Here, for the first time on its upward ascent, the soul knows itself as pure soul. It is here that true Self-realization is attained.

The "merchants" are the pure souls and the sea must be an allusion to the sea of 'nectar' or 'Living Water' which comprises a significant part of this region. It is in this 'pool' of Living Water, say the Masters, in which the souls 'bathe' after their release from the realms of the Mind. It is here that the last impressions of the Mind are finally washed away, the soul emerging as pure soul. 'Sea', 'pool', and 'bathe' are used metaphorically, of course, referring to a 'region' of purifying spirit, untainted by Mind and illusion. It is here that the soul can take its first real rest since it left the Lord.

In St John's gospel, as well as in other mystical literature of this period, the Word is commonly referred to as Living Water. This is an apt metaphor, for in a desert country it is apparent that, physically speaking, it is water which brings life. Just as the river Jordan runs through the desert, bringing life to all around, so too does the Word 'run' throughout the creation, bringing into being what we know of as life.

The "merchants" also refers to the Masters, for they are true merchants. A merchant is one who acts under the instructions of an owner. They are not the owners of the merchandise, but they have the full authority and trust of the owner to buy and sell on the owner's behalf. They are appointed by him to perform a particular task. So the Lord is the owner of this big business of creation, and the Masters are His merchants, His ambassadors, His agents.

The goods of this divine merchant are souls, and the wealth with which they are entrusted in order to carry out their work is the Word. From the physical creation, the Master 'purchases' the souls from the Universal Mind, the Negative Power. The payment given is the wealth of the Word. The souls are indebted to the Negative Power – their minds are still full of a myriad entanglements of karma, stored up from millions of past lives, sufficient to keep them in the Mind worlds forever. But the Lord wants certain souls released, sending His Sons as merchants to buy or ransom them from the Negative Power with the wealth of the Word.

However, although the Masters often say that they are the servants, ambassadors or merchants of God, this is only their humility. For in reality, Masters are identical with God Himself. So the souls are bought by the merchant of the Lord and taken to the Lord's own home, just as He had instructed. And there the souls realize that the one they had taken for a merchant is the Lord Himself.

THE INNER JOURNEY: SELF-REALIZATION

And my bright robe which I had stripped off,
And the toga wherein it was wrapped,
From the heights of Hyrcania,
My parents sent thither,
By the hand of their treasurers,
Who in their faithfulness could be trusted therewith.
But I remembered not the brightness of it;

For I was yet a child and very young,
When I had left it in the palace of my Father.
On a sudden as I faced it,
The garment seemed to me like a mirror of myself.
I saw in it my whole self,
Moreover I faced my whole self in facing it.
For we were two in distinction,
And yet again one in one likeness.

Here, the poet makes it quite clear that he is talking of the region where the soul attains Self-realization. The true garment of the soul, "woven to its stature", is its own true Self. This knowledge or gnosis it had lost when it descended into the creation.

It is only in Maishan, the region of Self-realization, that this "garment" or state of consciousness is restored to the soul. And the treasurer who brings the garment is, of course, the Master – now called the treasurer of the Lord. This treasure of true, mystical self-knowledge comes from the "heights of Hyrcania" – that is, from God. Geographically, Hyrcania was the high and mountainous region lying beyond Maishan, on the southern shores of the Caspian sea.

It is only the Masters, in their absolute and selfless dedication to the duty assigned to them by the Lord, who can "be trusted therewith" to bring the soul its own rightful treasure, its true spiritual heritage. Only they have the required degree of "faithfulness" – all other souls in the creation are caught up by the mind and as such serve their mind, their lower self, to a greater or lesser degree. It is not possible to serve the Lord completely until the mind is vanquished, for within the regions of the Mind one is utterly constrained to go where the inclinations, tendencies, attachments and entanglements of the mind take one. How then can one truly serve the Lord when one is constantly beholden to another, with no choice in the matter?

So it is a beautiful expression to say that only the treasurers, "in their faithfulness, could be trusted therewith." Only such faithful and trustworthy merchants can be entrusted to act as selfless Saviours, without any consideration of self-interest, to be given the wealth of the Word with which to 'purchase' souls from the Negative Power.

The treasurer, then, brings to the soul the garment of knowledge of its own true Self. And this is beautifully portrayed in the poem, for the soul, having forgotten the true nature of its divinely bestowed garment on its descent into the creation, when presented with it by the Master, sees in it its own Self, as in a mirror. It sees, its "whole self".

James translates this phrase as, "Saw it wholly in myself", which gives one the feeling that the original Syriac also contains the meaning of the soul becoming whole.

THE ONENESS OF THE TWO TREASURERS

Additionally, the soul observes:

And the treasurers also,
Who brought it to me, I saw in like manner,
That they were twain [yet of] one likeness.
For there was written on them [both],
The sign of the One King,
By Whose Hand, through them, were restored to me
My treasure and my wealth
And my bright embroidered robe.

The divergence between the various translations of this passage indicates the difficulties which the translators have encountered in deciphering the meaning. Yet the meaning is actually very clear and beautiful. The *two* treasurers, "twain [yet of] one likeness", are the Word and its personification, the Master. It is at this level that the soul sees and truly experiences for the first time that the Master and the Word are actually one and the same. Yet, though at long last the soul knows them to be one, all the same it still sees them as separate, hence: "Twain [yet of] one likeness."

In the regions of the Mind, the soul does not know itself as soul. It is striving for that knowledge or experience; it knows that it *will* have it; but it does not yet possess it. Nevertheless the mind and soul become utterly convinced that the great

Lord is within, though they have not yet experienced it. And, similarly, even in the Mind regions, the disciple also intuitively recognizes that the Master and the Word are one, but does not yet fully understand or know it.

Above the Mind, in the purely spiritual realms, understanding is yet again expanded. Here the soul perceives its own real nature. It comes to know its own true Self. Here the soul also understands more fully than ever before that the Master and the Word are one. Yet still, there is further to go before the realization is complete. Self-realization is only a step on the road to God-realization.

This is emphasized by the lines, "For there was written on them [both], the sign of the One King,"[1] indicating that both the Master and the Word are of the same kingly nature, that they are both of the Lord's essence, that He is the reality underlying them both.

And it is by the hand of these treasurers that the soul's treasure is restored to it. The soul of itself can do nothing. Only the Lord, the Word, and the Master can restore to the soul its own lost treasure and kingship.

THE RADIANT BEAUTY OF THE SOUL

Then the poet gives rein to his ecstasy in an attempt to describe the beauty of the soul and the Word in these regions of pure spirit. The treasurers, he says, restore to the soul:

My treasure and my wealth
And my bright embroidered robe,
Which was variegated with bright colours;
With gold and with beryls,
And rubies and agates
And sardonyxes varied in colour.
And skilfully worked in its home on high,
With diamond clasps, all its seams were fastened;

---

[1]The rendering here is supplied by the author in an attempt to make sense of the otherwise obscure translations, only light editing having been required.

And the image of the King of kings
Was depicted in full all over it,
And like the sapphire stone also were its manifold hues.

All mystics, in their descriptions of the higher regions, have
had no alternative but to describe the beauties and glories of
the soul in earthly terms, using as examples the most precious
and beautiful things that we earthly beings can understand. It
is not that the soul really wears gold and rubies, but that
its splendour and light are beyond description. And the source
of all this richness is "in its home on high", meaning with God.

An interesting metaphor is then presented. The garment is
sealed with "diamond clasps". Diamond is unbreakable and
here such a material is used to fasten all the seams. It refers
to the all-encompassing and indestructible experience of
Oneness. The garment has unbreakable seams. It is effectively
seamless – that is, it is a garment of Oneness. Similarly, Jesus
is said to have possessed a seamless garment, referring most
probably to his mystical attributes rather than his physical
attire – though the mystical metaphor has been misunder-
stood and externalized by later interpreters.

"And the image of the King of kings was depicted in full all
over it," signifies that it is apparent, at this stage of
consciousness, that the essence or real "image" of the soul is
the "King of kings", the Lord.

ON THE THRESHOLD OF HIS KINGDOM

Again I saw that all over it
The instincts [first beginnings] of knowledge
    [gnosis] were stirring,
And as if to speak I saw it also making itself ready.

[Then] I heard the sound of its voice,
Saying, "This thou art;[1]

---

[1]In these three lines, the translators again express their perplexity. A
rendering is offered here which draws together the meaning of their various
efforts.

> And for my sake it is that the treasurers have raised you,
> To usher you into the presence of my Father."

As the Creative Word leaves the Lord, the first movements or whirls of differentiation come into play. These are the 'seeds' that on further descent become the illusion of the Mind worlds. Where there is oneness, there is no motion, neither is there any knowledge, for knowledge implies a separation of the knower and the known, and motion indicates differentiation, a here and a there. The poet, therefore, is here describing the spiritual realm lying upon the threshold of the kingdom of God. "The instincts [first beginnings] of knowledge [gnosis] were stirring," he writes. The descent into creation has commenced.

But for the soul rising up, its source is now in sight as a bright and beckoning radiance upon the horizon. "This thou art," says the voice of the 'robe', meaning that the Word is the essence, the life principle, the true Self, within. Now the soul not only knows itself as pure soul but is beginning to realize its oneness with God.

It is "for my sake", says the 'robe', "that the treasurers have raised you," and brought you home. Only for the sake of the essence has the essence been gathered in. The Lord is playing the game of love with Himself alone, for He is in the soul and the soul is in Him. The soul was sent out by Him; the treasurers were sent out by Him. And He was and is within again them all, always. Never for a moment is He absent from the drama.

The royal robe, then, is both the soul – the real Self – and also the Word. The two are ultimately one. And the Master, too, is also one with the Word, one with the soul. As the soul rises up from the land of Maishan where it first received Self-realization, the consciousness of this oneness is increasingly felt. The intense longing of the soul to merge into its source, first felt as it awakened in the land of Egypt, intensifies as it realizes its proximity to the Lord.

> And I also perceived in myself
> That my stature was growing
> According to his [their?] labours.

There is some ambiguity in the translation at this point but the meaning seems to be that the Word is the doer, the active and vital principle in all things. It is the Word which administers and oversees the evolution and spiritual growth of the soul. And the Word is again identified with the treasurer, for the soul's stature grows "according to his [their?] labours." The soul cannot take egocentric credit for its spiritual growth, for it is the Word or Master who is arranging and doing everything. At best, the disciple can only become a willing puppet in his hands. "His [their?]" could be referring to the Lord, to the Master, or to the Word or, since they are all one, to all three. But either way, the meaning is the same.

> And in its kingly motions
> It was spreading itself out towards me,
> And in the hands of its givers
> It hastened that I might take it.

The Word with its compelling majesty and glory draws the soul ever closer to itself. It is the Word which is the prime mover. The soul only responds – with love and longing. But the source of this love is the Word itself. "It hastened that I might take" the garment, says the poet. The Word, the Master, is more anxious than his disciples about their spiritual progress.

THE REUNION OF THE SOUL: GOD-REALIZATION

> And love urged me on
> That I should run to meet it and receive it;
> And I stretched [myself] forth and received it,
> With the beauty of its colours I adorned myself
> And in my royal robe excelling in beauty
> I arrayed myself, wholly.

So the soul, impelled by the force of love and longing rushes forward and eagerly opens itself to the full reception of the robe. Firstly, the soul had seen its own image in the robe. It had seen that the two were one, but the full merging had not yet been consummated. Now the soul takes the robe and becomes fully clothed with it, is wholly covered by it. Mystically, this means that the soul finally merges with the Word as it enters the abode of God.

> I clothed myself therewith, and ascended
> To the gate of salutation and homage;
> I bowed my head and did homage
> To the Majesty of my Father who had sent it to me.

The soul reaches and enters the gateway of God, inwardly bowing in natural awe, reverence, worship and love. This is the true and spontaneous love and worship of the soul for God, having little or nothing to do with the set forms of worship and ritual we find in the temples, churches, and other man-made buildings of this world.

It is here that the soul discovers that the Master, the Word, the Lord and the soul itself are all one and the same. For it is here that the merging takes place. This is the true home of the soul. That is why the poet says that it was this "Majesty of the Father" who had sent the Word, the letter, to the soul.

So it is here that the soul directly experiences what it had previously understood only intuitively: that the Master is one with both the Father and the Word, that the Three are in the One and the One is in the Three. It is only here that the true nature of the trinity is actually understood and experienced. And no amount of theological hairsplitting, discussion, discoursing, argument or dogma can ever take the place of this sublime and utterly transcendental experience.

> For I had done his commandments,
> And he too had done what he had promised.

This union takes place because the soul had implicitly followed the instructions of the mystic 'letter' – had been guided by the Word and the Master. And the Father, too, had made good his promise, that if the soul went down into Egypt, took a human birth, and returned with the pearl, then it could

once again wear the seamless robe of divine love that most
befits a soul.

Yet it is also evident that the soul has only "done his
commandments" because the Master, the Father, so willed it.
Without the Master and the Creative Word, the soul would
still be lying fast asleep in Egypt!

> And at the gate of his princes
> I mingled with his nobles;
> For he rejoiced in me and received me,
> And I was with him in his kingdom.
> And with the voice all his servants glorify him.

So the soul reaches the kingdom of God, mingling there with
the other souls who inhabit that region, living in a state
of intoxicating worship and love of the Lord, blissfully
glorifying Him through the "Voice", the unending ringing
of the Divine Music of the Word. The drop has joined the
ocean.

But even this is not the end, for there are higher phases of
the Godhead to be experienced. Perfect mystics have said that
the Godhead is absolute and eternal, beyond all change and
dissolution. He is one, they say, yet He also has four aspects.
Firstly, there is that of the True Father, the "Majesty of my
Father". This phrase, in the original Syriac, is actually more
than simple descriptive praise. It refers to the first phase of the
Godhead, the True Father. But then, the Lord has three
further phases which one could call the Unknowable, the
Ineffable and the Formless Light. This is difficult to under-
stand with our human intellect, for how can unutterable
Oneness possess aspects or phases? Yet something of this
nature is clearly described here by our mystic poet. It is also
found in the writings of many other mystics, both of this and
other times. He says:

> And he promised that also to the gate
> Of the King of kings I should speed with him,
> And bringing my gift and my pearl
> I should appear with him before our King.

The Master, now revealed as the True Father of the soul, himself speeds the soul onwards towards its final consummation, its meeting with the Nameless and Formless Lord, the sublime Ocean of Pure Being, the Infinite One at the heart of all things. Here, no words can describe the beauty and the glory. Nothing can convey the idea. All one can say is that at this fount of all holiness, Love plays the supreme part. It is all Love.

4

THE HERITAGE OF THE ROBE

A MYSTICAL HERITAGE FROM THE PAST

The Robe of Glory is no isolated example of mystical teaching, but is part of a rich heritage, linking the Jewish writers of the Wisdom literature (*Proverbs*, *Ecclesiastes*, *The Song of Songs*, *The Wisdom of Jesus Ben Sirach* etc.), the Essenes, the earliest Christians, the gnostics, the Mandaeans and many others. Even elements of Egyptian and Greek mystical expression, sometimes quite pronounced, can be discerned amongst these writings. And in later generations the same manner of allegorical expression and the same mystic teachings are found amongst the Sufis of Persia and the mystics of India.

Much of this ancient literature has been lost or destroyed over the course of the centuries: historically, neither the Christians nor the Muslims have been noted for their tolerance of others' beliefs. But enough has been preserved – often poorly, it is true – for us to ascertain the meaning of the original writer. Sometimes the original texts have been edited and worked into the fabric of a religion or sect; sometimes the only available manuscripts have holes in them where the papyrus or leather has disintegrated; sometimes only fragments of torn leaves remain, like the earliest records of the gospels. But from all these sources one hears the same message.

In the remaining chapters of this book, therefore, some samples of these associated writings – as they relate to the allegory of *The Robe of Glory* – are presented.

THE MANICHAEAN CONNECTION

Bar Daisan lived in Syria around AD 155–233. Whether or
not he really wrote *The Robe of Glory* is not known: it is only
the poorly informed guess of scholarly research, for so little
remains of his life history and teachings. But what we do
know is that – together with many other mystics of this
period – he was castigated as a heretic by 'orthodox'
Christians.

Not long after Bar Daisan, however, there lived a mystic
whose teachings would appear to have been the same – at
least as those to be found in *The Robe of Glory* – and of
whom much more has been preserved, though whether the
two knew each other is unsure. His name was Mani and he
lived from about AD 215–277, spending his early years in
Mesopotamia or Persia. Mani gathered disciples around him
from as far to the east as India, perhaps even China, to as far
west as Rome – though this may also have been the work of
several successors. And he taught that Zarathushtra, Buddha
and Jesus had all been saviours, but that a soul continues in
the labyrinth of successive births and deaths until such time as
it meets a living saviour and attains salvation through him. He
was also vegetarian and drank no alcohol, teaching his
disciples likewise.

That Mani, too, had a Master, we can ascertain from his
own hand:

> A thankful disciple am I,
> Risen from Babel's land.
> Risen am I from the land of Babel,
> And standing [now] at the door of Truth.

MM p. 24/SCMP p. 114

Though Mani had a number of successors, the religion which
inevitably formed around their teachings after their departure
became a strong contender to Christianity. And most interest-
ingly, the Manichaeans of the fourth century adopted the *Acts
of Thomas* (in which *The Robe of Glory* is to be found),
together with the apocryphal *Acts of John, Andrew, Peter* and

Paul, as containing valuable material. Indeed, some scholars have maintained that *The Robe of Glory* is of Manichaean origin, though so little of the history is left that it is all a matter of conjecture. Like the canonical gospels and Acts, we do not possess copies of the manuscripts as they were at that time or when first written and thus cannot tell how much modification and editing they have undergone since their inception.

But although the greater part of Mani's writings have been lost or destroyed, some beautiful examples of his teachings still remain, samples of which are reproduced below, taken from *The Manichaean Hymn-Cycles in Parthian* translated by Mary Boyce, and from some other sources. They have been very lightly edited in a few places where the meaning seemed obscure or the phraseology too tortuous.

Bar Daisan, Mani and many others, including Jesus and John the Baptist, were representative of the many mystics who took birth in Greece, Egypt, Palestine, Syria and other countries of the Middle East in those ancient times. As one would expect amongst members of allied cultures and of the same era, there are great similarities in their manner of expression.

When I had repeated these words,
With soul a-tremble,
I beheld the Saviour as he shone before me.
I beheld the sight of all the Helmsmen,
Who had descended with him to array my soul.
I lifted up my eyes towards that direction,
And saw all deaths were hidden by the Envoy.

All ravages had become remote from me,
And grievous sickness,
And anguish of their distress.
The sight of them was hidden,
Their darkness fled away.
All was divine nature, without peer.

There shone forth light, elating and lovely,
And full of gladness,
Pervading all my mind.

In joy unbounded he spoke with me,
Raising up my soul from deep affliction: . . .

"From each dungeon shall I release thee,
Bearing thee afar from all wounds and afflictions.
I shall lead thee forth from this torture,
Thou shalt no more feel fear at each encounter.

"Beloved, beauty of my bright nature!
From these shall I lead thee forth,
And from all prisons.
I shall save thee from all perdition,
And free thee forever from all wounds.

"Through perfect Light,
I shall cleanse from thee
All the filth and corrosion
That thou hast passed through.
I shall deliver thee from all the waves of the sea,
And from its deep wherein
Thou hast gone through these drownings.

"I shall not wish to leave thee longer
In the hands of the Sinner
   [the Wicked One, Satan];
For thou art my own, in truth, for ever.

"Thou art the buried treasure,
The chief of my wealth,
The pearl which is the beauty of all the gods. . . ."

"You shall put on a radiant garment,
And gird on Light;
And I shall set on your head
The diadem of sovereignty. . . ."

"With power shall I carry thee,
Enfolding thee with love,
And lead thee to thy home, the Blessed Abode.

"For eternity shall I show to thee
  the noble Father;
I shall lead thee in, into His presence,
  in pure raiment.
I shall show to thee the Mother
  of the beings of Light.
For ever shalt thou rejoice in lauded happiness."

"I shall reveal to thee the holy Brethren,
The noble ones, who are filled with happiness. . . ."

"Fear and death shall never overtake thee more,
Nor ravages, distress and wretchedness.
Rest shall be thine in the place of salvation,
In the company of all the pure ones,
And those who dwell in peace."

MHCP pp. 139–147, 101, 153

The morning-light and dawn is come,
The radiant Light from the East;
Majestically has appeared
The sovereign God Narisah.

ML p. 138

You are praised and living, wakeful and eternal.
Your sign, your Self,
Your aspect is our beneficent Father,
The beautiful East, who is the form and appearance,
The aspect and power of the Father.

B, ML p. 142

You are longed for amongst the [spiritually] destitute,
You come to give salvation,
A treasure of jewels that you collect, is theirs;
At all times, you lead your sons upwards.
You are the Sovereign
Who gives as a present, the diadem.

ML p. 139

And all his friends – he binds the diadem upon them,
And clothes their bodies in the garment of bliss.

MHCP p. 103

They go to the heaven of Light . . .
They receive as their nature
The original splendour of the radiant palace
And are joyful.
They put on the resplendent garment,
And live forever in Paradise.

SP, ML p. 138

They are happy in the Light and know no pain.
All who enter there, stay for eternity.
Neither blows nor torture ever come upon them.

The garments which they wear, none has made by hand.
They are clean and bright,
Nothing of the earth is in them, [*lit.* no ants are in them].
Their verdant garlands never fade,
And they are wreathed brightly, in numberless colours.

Heaviness and drooping do not exist in their bodies,
And paralysis does not affect any of their limbs.

Heavy sleep never overtakes their souls,
And deceptive dreams and delusions
Are unknown among them.

MHCP p. 67–69

THE MANDAEANS AND NAZORAEANS

It is commonly thought by scholars that Mani was born into
a Mandaean family. The Mandaeans were a gnostic sect of
Jewish ancestry who moved to Mesopotamia in the early or
perhaps pre-Christian era, yet managed to survive until the
present century in the marshlands of Iran and Iraq. *Manda*

means mystic knowledge or gnosis and their name for themselves is *Mandaiia*, meaning 'gnostics'. Those amongst them considered to have achieved this gnosis, they call *Nasuraiia* – 'Nazorenes' or 'Nazoraeans', from the term *Nazirutha*, which covers a wide range of meaning including mystic enlightenment, and the power (the Word) by which such a state of consciousness is achieved, as well as the associated mystic teachings. The closest word in English is probably 'Truth', in all its various connotations.

Some idea of the antiquity of the Mandaeans can be gleaned from the fact that there are passages in their sacred writings which reflect those found at Qumran, the pre-Christian Dead Sea site of the Essenes, as well as those reminiscent of the Jewish Wisdom literature. The Mandaeans also acknowledged John the Baptist, amongst many others, as one of their spiritual preceptors, some of their traditions seeming to indicate that their ancestors may have moved to Mesopotamia, due to persecution, during the time or shortly after that of John the Baptist. It also appears likely that John the Baptist had a far longer and more wide-ranging ministry than is generally presumed from the very brief references made to him in the Christian gospels. Incidentally, the Mandaean language itself is Semitic in character, being a modern version of Aramaic, a further indication of their early roots.

The origin of the appellation, 'Nazorene', though a side issue in this context, raises some intriguing lines of thought, for Jesus and his disciples were called Nazarenes or Nazoraeans. Even today, the Quran and Muslim religious writings refer to the Christians as Nasara. Yet the term is said by the church father, Epiphanius, to have been in use before Jesus.

In the *Acts of the Apostles*, one of the earliest texts concerning the Christian religion, Paul is described as "a ringleader of the sect of the Nazarenes" (*Acts 24:5*), and the term is also found in *St Matthew 2:23* as a description of Jesus: "He shall be called a Nazarene." (Though this statement is said by the gospel writer to be a quotation from "scripture" – the Old Testament – no one has ever found any trace of it.)

Similarly, the phrase "Jesus of Nazareth", encountered in

Acts 22:8 and again in *St Mark 1:23*, is better translated as "Jesus the Nazarene", as it is in some well-respected translations of the New Testament.

In any event, the early Church fathers, many of whom were Greek-speaking, called themselves Christians, a Greek term which arose in the non-Jewish world. And they spoke of the Nazorenes, often disparagingly, as a Judaeo-Christian sect, transliterating the word from Hebrew into Greek as Nazarenes, Nazoraeans, Nasoraeans, and other variants.

In the popular mind, it has always been tacitly understood that Jesus was called a Nazarene because he came from Nazareth. But most philologists consider that the form found in St Matthew and Acts could not mean "of Nazareth". Some scholars have also pointed out that there is no reference to Nazareth as a village until the fourth century AD, even suggesting that some other village was later renamed to fit the legend.

In fact, the Jewish historian Josephus (died AD 101), who knew the area well, being governor of Galilee, wrote a detailed account of the province, but never once mentioned Nazareth. Neither is a village of that name ever mentioned in the Old Testament. And in any case, sects or religions were not usually named after a village or locality. By the early fourth century, however, when Constantine, the first Christian Roman Emperor, ordered a listing of all places held to be holy by the Christians, it seems that there was a village of Nazareth in Galilee, no doubt catering to the growing traffic of pilgrims.

Whatever may be the truth of the matter, it is clear from his teachings that Jesus was a mystic, a true man of God, a Nazorene or Nazarene, in the Mandaean sense. And it is as probable a solution to the enigma as any other, to say that Jesus had attained *Nazirutha*, perfect spiritual enlightenment, and that he also taught that path to others. Jesus and his disciples, then, were Nazarenes or Nazoraeans: followers of the mystic path to God, though the real links between John the Baptist, Jesus, and the Mandaeans can still only be surmised.

This conclusion appears to be clinched by two passages

from *Gospel of Philip*, one of the writings found in the Nag Hammadi region of upper Egypt in 1944. There, the unknown author says:

> 'Jesus' is a private name. Christ is a public name [epithet]. For this reason 'Jesus' is not particular to any language; rather he is always called by the name 'Jesus'. But the word for 'Christ' in Syriac is 'Messiah', and in Greek it is 'Khristos', and probably all the others have it according to the particular language of each. 'The Nazarene' is he who reveals what is hidden.

Gospel of Philip 56:3–13, NHL p. 144, GS p. 332

> The apostles before us used to employ the terms: 'Jesus the Nazoraean Messiah', which means 'Jesus, the Nazoraean, the Christ [anointed one]'. The last name is 'Christ', the first name is 'Jesus', the middle name is 'the Nazarene'.

> 'Messiah' has two meanings, 'Christ [anointed one]' and 'the measured'. 'Jesus' in Hebrew means 'the redemption'. 'Nazara' means 'the truth', thus 'the Nazarene' means 'truth'.

Gospel of Philip 62:8–15, NHL p. 147, GS p. 332

A meeting point of ancient mystic teachings, the Mandaean scriptures make a fascinating study, for the literary allusions of the past mystic schools of the Middle East, including Zoroastrianism, Judaism, early Christianity and Manichaeism are all to be found therein. The imagery of *The Robe of Glory* is also well represented, as one would expect when one considers its Christian and Manichaean connections.

The Mandaeans had many names for God, but probably the most commonly encountered is Great Life, House of Life, or simply Life, meaning the Source of all Being and Existence. Like the Manichaean sources previously quoted, this is not the place for a full presentation of their writings, but certain poems stand out as particularly relevant to *The Robe of Glory* and are reproduced below. All quotations are taken either from *The Canonical Prayerbook of the Mandaeans*, translated by E.S. Drower, or from *The Secret Adam* by the same author.

A Saviour will come forth towards you.
The Saviour that cometh towards you
Is all radiancy and light from head to foot
Like the wreath in his right hand.

And on his two arms is a robe.
Bestir yourselves! Put on your robes!
Put on your living wreaths . . .
In which nothing is awry or blemished.

CPM p. 54

The soul remaineth and waiteth
  in the hostel of the body . . .
Till its measure and count were accomplished.

When its measure and count were accomplished
The Deliverer came to her;
To her came the Deliverer
Who loosed her and bore her away:
Yea, he who had bound [baptized] her,
Who had loosed the soul,
Went before her whom he had bound.

Coming behind him the soul hasted,
Reached her Deliverer, ran after him . . .

The soul and her Deliverer go:
Her course is to the place of Light,

To the place whose sun goeth not down,
Nor do its lamps of light grow dim.
To it, and to that place,

Those souls that are called . . .
And signed by this sign [marked and baptized],
Are summoned and invited.

They shall behold the great Place of Light
And the Abiding Abode.

CPM p. 55

The voice of the Framer of Bodies
   [Satan, Universal Mind] is heard . . .
And he saith to the soul,

"Go in peace, daughter of the free . . .
Go in peace, pure Pearl that was transported
From the Treasuries of Life;
Go in peace, fragrant one
Who imparted her fragrance to the stinking body.
Go in peace, radiant one,
Who illumined her dark house [of the body].
Go in peace, pure and chosen one,
Immaculate and spotless!"

Flying, the soul went
Until she reached the House of Life:
She arrived at the House of Life.

Pure souls went forth towards her,
Saying to her,
"Take and put on thy robe of radiance
And set on thy brow, thy living wreath!
Arise, dwell in these realms,
The place where the pure abide."

CPM p. 56

Behold! This is the Pearl
Which came and gave them light!

She it is who maketh your stink fragrant!
If you do not desire her,
She will not remain with you!

SA p. 55

A sealed letter . . .
A letter written in good faith
And sealed with the seal of the Mighty One –
Holy men [Saviours] wrote it,
Men of faith [Saviours] tied it on,
And suspending it about the soul's neck,
They despatched it to the Gate of Life.

The soul, in her wisdom,
Pressed her nail [signet, essence?] on the letter
    [she merged herself with it].
Her nail she pressed on the letter;
She imbued it with her mystic radiance,
Wrapped it and veiled it in her light . . .

The soul flieth and goeth
Until she reacheth the House of Life.
When she reached the House of Life
She uttered a cry to the House of Life,
And when He heard her call,
The House of Life sent a Messenger towards her,
Who grasped her by the palm of her hand,
Conducted her, supported her,
In the likeness of Life Itself,
To the place of radiance,
Light and beams of effulgence;

To unite her with the company of the pure ones,
And to set her up amongst beams of light.

CPM pp. 61–62

May the vivifying power of Life rest upon us.
My elect, ye shall say,
"Blessed be the Voice of Life [the Creative Word]
And praised be the great Beam [the Creative Word]
Which is all light!"

CPM p. 57

The Crown [Godhead] is composed of four mysteries,
Which are the Wellspring [Source of Living Water],
    and Date Palm [True Father],
Fecundity [Immanent Creative Potential],
Glory [Ineffability] and Light [Formless Radiant Source].

SA p. 9

What did thy Father do for thee, Soul,
The great day on which thou wast
Raised up [from death in the body]?
"He took me down to the Jordan
    [the Living Waters, the Creative Word],
Planted me [baptized me],
And rose and stood me upon its bank
    [rescued me from the creation].

"He broke and gave me [the] bread [of Life],
Blessed the cup and gave me thereof to drink
    [from the Living Waters].
He placed me between his knees,
    [he took me under his protection],
And pronounced over me the name of the Mighty Life
    [he put me in contact with the Name of God,
    initiated me].

"He passed into the mountain before me,
    [he ascended into the inner realms].
He cried loudly that I might hear
    [the Creative Word],

That I might hear he cried loudly,
'If there is strength in thee, Soul, come!'

"[And I replied], 'If I climb the mountain
    [if I go inside] I shall fall,
I shall overturn and perish from the world!'
    [She expresses her sense of ineptitude.]
But I lifted my eyes to heaven
    [I focused my attention inside],
And my soul waited upon the House of Life
·   [travelling inwards upon the current of the Word].
I climbed the mountain and fell not.
I came and found the life of my Self
    [I reached the region of Self-realization]. . . ."

"I go forth towards my Counterpart
    [my highest Self, God, the Source of Life]
And my Counterpart cometh out toward me,
It fondleth and embraceth me
As if I had come from prison
    [the physical universe].

"Life had supported Life:
Life had found its own:
It hath found its own,
And my soul hath found
That for which she had yearned."

                                        SA pp. 53–55

The Great Life hath stretched forth
His right hand to thee!
Put away passion from thy thought!
Thy thought shall be filled with Ours
And thy garment (*mana*) and our Garment (*Mana*)
Shall become one.

                                        SA p. 55

There is an interesting play on words here ("garment" and "Garment"), relevant to *The Robe of Glory* and pointed out by E.S. Drower in *The Secret Adam*. Mandaean, though a Semitic language derived from Aramaic, has absorbed many words from its Persian and Mesopotamian environment. In Aramaic, *mana* means 'a garment', 'robe', or 'vessel'. But in Iranian, *Mana* means the First Power, the First Cause, even the First 'Thought' or Creative 'Mind', in the sense of Primal Essence or Essence of Being. It is therefore another term for the Word. It is equivalent to the Greek mystic term, *Nous*, usually translated by scholars as 'Mind', though often used as a reference to the Word.

In *The Robe of Glory* the word appears to be used with a double meaning, which becomes clear in the poem at the stage where the soul reaches the regions above the level of the Universal Mind. For there, the garment or vessel (*mana*), symbolic of the soul, the true self, becomes one with the robe or Word (*Mana*) that is sent from on high. The soul and the Word become one – as they are in the word *mana*. The Valentinian gnostics are also said to have described the soul as "a precious vessel (*mana*)."

THE ZOROASTRIAN CONNECTION

Mani taught that Zarathushtra (the later Greeks called him Zoroaster), who lived around 1500 BC, had also been a Saviour, a true Apostle – a divine Messenger sent by God to redeem these souls given into his care. Certainly, a study of Zarathushtra's *gathas* (poetry) reveals that the essential elements of all such Masters are indeed present in his teachings. And since Zoroastrianism was still a major religion in Iran and the surrounding areas in the time of Jesus and Mani, it is understandable that Mani and other mystics would have brought out the real meaning of Zarathushtra's teachings which had been obscured by the processes of religion. They would also have used his examples, parables and allegories.

For this reason, in both Manichaean and Mandaean literature, we find a number of metaphors and mystic terms that are used by Zarathushtra or are found in later Zoroastrian writings. One of these is *Vohu Mana*, often somewhat vaguely translated by scholars as 'Good Mind', although it is actually one of the terms used by Zarathushtra in reference to the creative and loving power of God in the creation. In the Zoroastrian writings of the *Denkart*, for instance, *Vohu Mana* is described as "visiting" the soul:

> Every opening of the [inner] eye
> [Comes to pass] by the complete visiting of *Vohu Mana*
> To the life principle [the soul].
>
> *Denkart ed. Madan, p. 281, GVMAG p. 46*

Geo Widengren also writes in *The Great Vohu Manah and the Apostle of God*:

> It is related in a passage in *Datastan i denik* [another Zoroastrian writing] that the soul of the righteous man [the devotee], accompanied by the good spirit who is the 'companion of the soul' after death, ascends to the heavenly abodes and to the garment. . . . And having introduced the soul to Ahura Mazda [the Supreme Lord], *Vohu Mana* shows it its throne and reward.
>
> *GVMAG pp. 49–50*

And in the same Zoroastrian book, *Vohu Mana* is likened to a seamless garment, a metaphor with which we have become familiar:

> It is necessary that it is the healthy, white, pure,
> Single [garment], made in one piece,
> Just as *Vohu Mana* is in this manner
>   the first creature [created power].
> Consequently, it is from him [*Vohu Mana*]
> That . . . the innermost and concealed garment
>   has its appellation.
>
> *Datastan i denik 40:2, GVMAG p. 50*

Again, in the *Denkart*, reference is made to:

> The light and white garment . . .
> [Which is] the very selfness of Ohrmizd [Ahura Mazda],
> His garment and his brilliance.

Denkart ed. Madan, p. 204, GVMAG p. 50

In all cases, therefore, the references in *The Robe of Glory* to the seamless robe or garment as the true essence or self of the soul, being one with the Creative Word, are to be found in the Mandaean, Manichaean and far earlier Zoroastrian writings. Indeed, the dual meaning of the term pointed out by E.S. Drower is also present, for man's physical form is also referred to as a garment. The *Datastan i denik*, for example, speaks of:

> The wearing of flesh,
> Which is the garment of the visible world.

Datastan i denik 37:33 (25), GVMAG p. 51

Many of the mystic metaphors and parables, used in turn by Jewish mystics in the Wisdom literature and in the Old Testament generally, by Jesus, by the Mandaeans, by Mani, and by the many mystics or gnostics of the ancient Middle East, are traceable, historically, to Zarathushtra. Before that, we find fragments of the same manner of mystical expression upon the clay tablets preserved for over 4,000 years from the ancient Sumerian culture; and in later times, we find the same metaphors being used amongst the great Sufis of Islam and the mystics of India. This, indeed, is worthy of a full study in itself, for both the Old as well as the New Testaments are greatly illuminated thereby. Mystics always express the same perennial truths. They describe the same eternal mystic reality. And in the process they use the extant language, teachings, expressions and examples of their predecessors – those in whom the people they are teaching have faith or whose teachings have become a religion.

ADAM AND THE LETTER

In the following Mandaean passage, the "mystery" being
described is *Adam Kasia*, *Adam Qadmaia* or *Adam Kadmon*
– the Cosmic Man, or Essence of Man, which signifies the
essence of the soul, the Word. The "Good Man" is the
personification of this power, a living Master, who can give
each disciple his personal attention.

> For this mystery, this explanation,
> Is a Voice which explaineth voices,
> A Word which interpreteth all words:
> It is a Good Man who teacheth,
> Addressing each individually.

SA p. 22

Mystic contact with the Voice or Word brings an under-
standing of all mysteries to the soul. It is a Good Man who
personally imparts this wisdom and guides the soul.

The allegory goes on to describe the creation of the Cosmic
Adam, the Word, as the Firstborn Son of God, the first and
primary creative emanation. As the Cosmic Adam, the Word,
descends through the higher realms of creation 'he' ultimately
comes to the physical universe, becoming the soul of man.
The tale then continues:

Then he [Adam] arose
And sat by a well of vain imaginings,
   [he became a normal human being, lost in his ego],
And said, "I am a king without peer!
I am lord of the whole world!"

He travelled on into all the world
Until he came and rested on a mountain,
Then he gazed about and perceived a Stream
Coming from beneath the mountain.

Then he prostrated himself,
Cast himself down on his face and said,

"Is there [then] a loftier and mightier than I?
This is a stream of Living Waters,
White [pure] waters which come
From worlds without limit or count!"

Then his mind became disquieted.
He pondered and said,
"I said that there was no king greater than I,
But now I know that there exists
That which is greater than myself.
I pray that I may see him
And take him for my Companion.

Then a Voice came from above
At which he fell upon his face
And was powerless to rise
And stayed fallen on his face
Until Ayar-Dakia [Pure Spirit] came –
And in his right hand he was carrying a Letter.

Then Adam took the Letter into his right hand,
Smelt at it, sneezed, prayed [meditated]
And praised the King who is all Light and said,
"I beseech Thee for lofty strength like Thine own."

SA p. 25–26

In Semitic folklore, sneezing is indicative of having awakened – for only a wakeful person will sneeze!

Then a Voice came to him from above
And it sent Mahzian-the-Word.
In his hand he was carrying a Letter.
And he came towards him
And gave the Letter into Adam's right hand
And Adam kissed it three hundred and sixty times,
Then opened it,
But understood not what was in it.
But he rejoiced in his mind
And prostrated himself before Mahzian-the-Word

And thereafter arose
And understood the ABG [equivalent to our ABC]
And, little by little, comprehended all Nazirutha.

SA p. 26

Reading through these passages from the Manichaean and Mandaean literature, one is struck by their similarity, both to each other as well as to *The Robe of Glory*. We seem to be looking at fragments of an ancient mystic teaching, scattered by time, by persecution and by human inability to understand and value the simple, common message.

Yet that same message is being taught even in our present times. The guise and the language may change, but the world is never without at least one living Master. And his role never changes.

5

REFLECTIONS OF THE ROBE

A MYSTIC LETTER
IN THE *ODES OF SOLOMON*

Just as *The Robe of Glory* is to be found embedded in the midst of an unlikely romantic 'history' of the apostle Thomas, so too are many other spiritual or mystic truths – often beautifully expressed – to be found in the non-canonical literature.

Some are in the form of short discourses or poems, or paraphrases of traditional mystic sayings and allegories, perhaps not fully understood even by the compiler of the text we have before us. While in other instances, entire books, treatises or poems of pure and unadulterated material have survived. An excellent example is the *Odes of Solomon*. These forty-two poems are beautiful and deeply mystical, showing little evidence of later editorial tampering. Similarly, amongst the gnostic literature, both of the Egyptian Nag Hammadi find earlier this century, as well as in the writings previously known, there is much mystic truth and beauty. This is all our heritage, as members of a Christian culture that takes its religious roots from the Middle East. It is the purpose of the remaining chapters, therefore, to present this material, inasmuch as it relates to the imagery and teachings of *The Robe of Glory*.

In *The Robe of Glory*, the Word is portrayed as a letter which comes from God to the physical universe to redeem the fallen soul. In *Ode XXIII* of the *Odes of Solomon* (AOT

p. 713–714), the same similes are used, with the difference
that the physical universe, instead of being portrayed as Egypt
or as a labyrinth, is symbolized as a wheel – the wheel of birth
and death. The letter is manifested or revealed in the world as
the "Son of Truth", a Master, opening out a way for souls to
return to God. The poet says that all confusions and
diversions are clarified and dispelled when a Master comes
into the life of a human being. And the Word manifest in the
human form is succinctly described as, "the Head came down
to the feet."

The translation used is mainly that of J.A. Emerton in *The
Apocryphal Old Testament*, with some insertions from those
of J.H. Bernard, J.H. Charlesworth, and J.R. Harris. Three
lines are of my own rendering, where all the translators admit
their perplexity.

> Joy [bliss] belongs to the saints [devotees],
> And who will put it on but they alone?
> Grace belongs to the elect
>   [the initiates, the marked souls],
> And who will receive it but those
> Who have trusted in it from the beginning?
> Love belongs to the elect,
> And who will put it on but those
> Who have possessed it from the beginning?
> Walk in the knowledge of the Most High,
> And you will know [experience] the generosity
>   of the Lord's grace,
> His exultation [magnificence]
> And the perfection of His knowledge.

The poem begins with an exhortation to the soul, pointing out
that the highest divine love, grace and knowledge of the Lord
can only be realized by the "elect", by the "saints" or devotees
who are baptized. The terms "the elect" and "the saints" are
commonly found in Jewish and Christian mystical writings
for the disciples of a Master. God-realization can only be
attained through the grace of initiation by a perfect Master.
This does not mean, of course, that others can experience no
love or grace or mystic knowledge. This is manifestly not the

case. It is only that to attain the supreme *height* of such experience requires a living guide.

The gnostics and early Christians called such mystics the Living One, the Standing One, the Existing One, the Christ, the Messiah, the Apostle, the Envoy, the Messenger, the Saviour, the Redeemer, the Deliverer, the Friend of God, the Angel and, in the generous and lyrical style of the times, by many other names. In allusion to the many mystic parables of Jesus and others, the Master was also called the Pearl, the Great Fisherman, the Shepherd, the Sower of the Seed, the Merchant of God, the Treasurer, the Helmsman, and so on.

The assertion concerning the need of a living Master is commonly misunderstood as a sectarian and exclusive point of view and it is true that terms such as "the elect" tend to underline this interpretation. However, the need of a teacher in any other sphere of life should be readily acceptable. Chemistry students are not considered a sect through being taught by a particular professor – though they would be if they declared that their professor, especially if he was dead, was the only teacher from whom a correct knowledge of chemistry could be learnt. Knowledge of any kind – however universal – is always taught by someone, and is best gained by personal association with an expert. With mystic knowledge, this is particularly true.

When such terms are misunderstood and come to be applied to the followers of a particular religion or members of a particular nation, then sectarianism and division begin. But in this poem, the true nature of "the elect" is made very clear: only "the elect" will truly "walk in the knowledge of the Most High." Only they can become one with God, only they can actually *see* God within themselves. Jesus, whose love was universal and for all creation, also told his disciples: "I know my sheep, and am known of mine" (*St John 10:14*), "Ye have not chosen me, but I have chosen you" (*St John 16:16*), and "Ye are the salt of the earth" (*St Matthew 5:13*). And when speaking of the power of false prophets or masters to mislead others, he says, "For there shall arise false Christs and false prophets, and shall show great signs and wonders; insomuch that, if it were possible, they shall deceive the very elect" (*St Matthew 24:24*).

Disciples are destined for a particular Master and constitute the 'flock' for whom he has to care, but this does not make them into a sect. In fact, the disciples of a living Master have the potential to become the most universal of all people. They come to see God in all, to see Him working everywhere. So such designations do not imply any narrowing of a person's horizons. Rather, it is only these rare few who truly become free from the intolerance and prejudice of religious, national and social sectarianism.

> And His Thought [emanation] was like a letter,
> His Will descended from on high;
> And it was sent like an arrow from a bow,
> That is shot with force;
> And many hands rushed upon the letter,
> To seize it and to take it and to read it;
> And it fled from their fingers;
> And they were afraid of it and of the seal
>   which was upon it,
> Because they were not allowed to loose its seal,
> For the power that was upon the seal
>   was greater than they.
>
> But those who saw it went after the letter,
> That they might know where it would alight,
> And who would read it,
> And who would hear it.

The 'Thought' or Primary Emanation (the Word) of the Lord is likened to a letter, sent from on high like an "arrow from a bow that is shot with force." It is also compared to "His Will descending from on high", because it is by this power or force that everything in the creation is manifested.

Many souls observe the letter on its journey through the higher levels of creation and many wish to lay their hands on it, for they recognize its essential power. But it is not their part to do so. So, in the story, they follow it to see where it might stop – "and who would *hear* it." A letter that can be *heard* has become a familiar symbol from *The Robe of Glory* and here the poet also emphasizes that many souls in the higher realms of creation yearn for contact with the Letter or Word and one of its Messengers.

Like all areas of creation, the inner regions are densely populated with souls. There, it is clear to all that they are a part of the Lord's great creation and many wish to go higher and return to Him. It is in the design of creation, however, that this privilege is given only to a human being; it is only man's good fortune.

> But a Wheel received it,
> And the letter covered [overcame] it.
> For with the letter was a sign
> Of Kingship and Government.
>
> And everything that was moving the Wheel
> It mowed and cut down;
> It overwhelmed a multitude of adversaries;
> And it covered rivers with earth
>   [and stopped them flowing];
> And it crossed over [traversed]
> And uprooted many forests
> Making a broad [and open] path.
>
> The Head came down to the feet,
> For at the feet ran the Wheel,
> And whatever was turning on it.

At the end of its journey, it is received by a "Wheel" – the wheel or labyrinth of birth and death. The journey's end for the Word is the physical creation – this is the nethermost pole of creation. But it is also the point from which a soul can commence its return to God, after being signed and sealed by the "letter".

The letter arrives with the sign "of Kingship and Government", the 'signature' of God. The Word is His command. And "everything that was moving the Wheel" is "mowed and cut down." All the powers of the Mind that govern this world, all the powers of Satan, are conquered with the help of the Word. All adversaries – human weaknesses and all diversions of the mind – are overcome, "covered" or "overwhelmed" with the aid of the letter. The sound of the Inner Music is so sweet and captivating that the mind automatically abandons all lower tendencies and rises up from the body towards the Lord.

The rivers of human lust, anger, greed and pride, flowing uncontrollably, are dammed by the power of this "letter". It halts the otherwise incessant flow of the mind into the world of the physical senses and its consequent attachments and entanglements. Dark and tangled "forests" are traversed and "uprooted" by it: it "makes a broad path" of clarity amongst a maze of conflict and confusion. "The Head came down to the feet" – the Lord (the Head) appeared in the physical universe (the feet) as a personification of the Word, the living Master.

> The letter was one of command,
> And all realms were under its jurisdiction.
>
> And on its Head appeared the head that was revealed,
> Even the Son of Truth from the Most High Father,
> Whose inheritance is power over the entire creation.

The letter is also the Will of God, manifested in the creation. It is a letter "of command" and "all realms [are] under its jurisdiction." The Word is the power by which God creates and maintains the creation.

On the "Head" of the letter appears the head of the one "that was revealed" or manifested: "even the Son of Truth" – a living Master, the Word manifested in the flesh, whose inheritance is power over the entire creation, because a Master is one with the creative power of the Word.

> And the thoughts of the many came to nothing.
> And those who led [others] astray hasted and fled away.
> And the persecutors were extinguished and blotted out.

At his coming, his initiates were rescued from the multitudinous thoughts, religions and philosophies of the world. The false teachers and priests of the world, who incorrectly interpret the teachings of past mystics, could no longer exert any hold over them. And those who persecuted spiritual people were also left behind in this world. To the initiated souls, soaring high into the inner realms, they became as if they had never existed.

These lines of the poem also carry a double meaning, for in reality it is the myriad thoughts of our minds which lead us astray, and our own human weaknesses which persecute us and cause us suffering. At the coming of the Word as a Master into the life of an earthbound soul, all these human characteristics flee away, little by little, and are extinguished forever.

> And the letter was a great volume,
> Which was wholly written by the finger of God;
> And the Name of the Father was upon it,
> And of the Son, and of the Holy Spirit,
> To reign for ever and ever.
> Hallelujah.

The poem then ends by describing the letter as a huge 'book', for everything in the creation lies 'written' within this 'book', everything is created and continuously manifested by the Word.

And the letter is 'signed' by the "Father", "the Son", and the "Holy Spirit". That is: the letter carries the stamp and authority of God, the Master and the "Holy Spirit" or Word. The Holy Spirit and the Master are one with God: three-in-One and One-in-three. And it will always be this way, they will "reign for ever and ever". This is the continuous story of creation.

THE FOUR-FOLD GODHEAD

In *The Robe of Glory*, when the soul finally reaches the Majesty of the Father and merges with Him, it finds that it has yet further glory, light and love to experience:

> And he promised that also to the gate
> Of the King of kings I should speed with him,
> And bringing my gift and my pearl
> I should appear with him before our king.

In the commentary, it was remarked that mystics have said
that although the Godhead is unutterably and utterly One, yet
He also has aspects. Philosophically, this is almost impossible
to understand, for how can the Undifferentiated have any-
thing even remotely resembling differentiation? No doubt it is
a matter to be experienced, rather than understood by
intellect, but it is interesting to note that other mystics of this
same culture and period also spoke of the four aspects of the
Godhead. We have already seen that the Mandaeans held this
belief:

> The Crown [Godhead] is composed of four mysteries,
> Which are the Wellspring [Source of Living Water],
>   and Date Palm [True Father],
> Fecundity [Immanent Creative Potential],
> Glory [Ineffability] and Light [Formless, Radiant Source].

SA p. 9

And we find this same matter described in the gnostic
literature of Nag Hammadi. In the following passages,
Kalyptos is a name given to the Supreme Lord, and an "aeon"
is a power, a realm or a ruling lord. The distinction is also
made between that which "really exists" and the illusion and
impermanence of the creation. Only the Supreme Lord, in His
four-fold aspect, "really exists". He is the ultimate Reality. All
other realms in His creation are subject to change and
occasional dissolution. They are therefore unreal or illusory,
like a dance, a mirage or a play. Unfortunately, the manu-
script is very poorly preserved, leaving many words illegible
or missing:

> Kalyptos is a single aeon;
> He has four different aeons. . . .
> All of them exist in One, dwelling together. . . .
> And filled with the aeon which really exists. . . .
>
> The first of the aeons is Harmedon, the Father-Glory.
> The second Light is one in which He is unknowable. . . .
> The third Light is . . .

The fourth Light is . . . a teaching and glory . . .
and the Truth of the four aeons. . . .

The aeons which really exist do so in Silence.
The [Supreme] Existence was [is] inactivity,
And knowledge of the self-established Kalyptos
was [is] ineffable. . . .

Together with the aeon in the aeons,
He has a fourfold difference with all the rest
who are there.
But Kalyptos really exists. . . .
It is Kalyptos who has divided again,
And they exist together.

> *Zostrianos 115:14, 116:1–6, 120:2–5, 10–11,
> 18–19, 22–23, 124:14–19, 7–12, 121:5–6,
> NHL pp. 426–428*

There are many references in other gnostic writings – notably those attributed to a group designated the Sethians – to the four divisions of the Godhead, in particular *Marsanes* (NHL), *Allogenes* (NHL), the *Gospel of the Egyptians* (NHL), *A Valentinian Exposition* (NHL) and *Pistis Sophia*. However, the references are either vague, have obviously presented difficulties in translation resulting in considerable obscurity, or the manuscripts are in such poor condition that many words are illegible.

A number of gnostic writings, for instance, talk of the Silent One as the Triple-Powered One, referring to the three aspects 'beyond' what we have called the True Father. And the *Gospel of the Egyptians* refers to the Supreme Power as "the Four Lights":

The great Seth [their Saviour] was sent by the four lights. . . .

> *Gospel of the Egyptians 62:24–26, NHL p. 216*

THE MOTHER, THE MOUNTAIN AND THE LIGHT FORM OF THE MASTER

In *The Robe of Glory*, the Word or Holy Spirit is described as "thy Mother, the Mistress of the East". This common mystic metaphor of the times also appears in the *Teachings of Silvanus*, one of the Nag Hammadi treatises':

Accept Christ, this true Friend, as a good teacher.
Cast from you death, which has become a father to you.
For death did not exist, nor will it exist at the end.

But since you cast yourself from God –
The holy Father, the true Life, the Spring of Life –
Therefore you have obtained death as a father
And have acquired ignorance as a mother.
They have robbed you of the true knowledge.

But return, my son, to your first Father, God,
And Wisdom your Mother,
From whom you came into being from the very first
In order that you might fight against all of your enemies,
The powers of the Adversary.

Teachings of Silvanus 90:33, 91:1–20, NHL p. 384

Here, God is portrayed as the "holy Father, the true Life, the Spring of Life", while Wisdom, or the Word, is the true "Mother, from whom you came into being from the very first", and through whom the "enemies" of the soul can be fought and vanquished. These "enemies" are the agents or "powers of the Adversary", Satan, the Universal Mind, manifested at the human level as the weaknesses of our own minds.

But in this world, says the writer, everything is reversed. We have acquired death as a father and ignorance as a mother, and these false 'parents' have robbed us of the true knowledge and experience of God. In fact, he says, death is an illusion, it does not really exist and, ultimately, it will be realized that death does not exist, for the soul is immortal, surviving bodily death. Though the soul may continue to revolve in the labyrinth of birth and death, it is only the body which dies, only the garment or skin is changed. The soul never dies.

Jerome (AD ?347–?420) and other early church fathers tell us that there was once a *Gospel According to the Hebrews* which closely resembled yet also possessed significant differences from our Greek *Gospel According to St Matthew*. It was written in Hebrew characters, in the Aramaic or Hebrew language, and was used by the Nazarenes or Nazoraeans.

The text has long since been lost, and is extant only as a handful of brief Greek citations in the writings of Jerome and others, but there we find, quoted by Origen in the early third century:

> Even now did my Mother, the Holy Spirit,
> Take me by one of mine hairs,
> And carried me away to the great mountain Thabor.

> *Gospel According to the Hebrews, ANT p. 2*

The Holy Spirit is again described as the "Mother" of the soul, and in this excerpt we also see how mountains are symbolic of the inner regions. The soul is carried high up into the inner regions, cradled and merged into the Holy Spirit like a little child in the arms of its mother.

Similarly, in the *Acts of Peter*, we find Peter saying:

> Our Lord, willing that I should behold
> His majesty in the holy mount . . .
> I . . . saw the brightness of his light,
> Fell as one dead and shut mine eyes,
> And heard such a Voice from him
> As I am not able to describe,
> And thought myself to be blinded
>   by his brightness. . . .

And he gave me his hand and raised me up;
And when I arose I saw him again
In such a form as I was able to take in.

Acts of Peter III:XX, ANT p. 321

The "holy mount" means on the inner planes. There, Peter
sees the light form of his Master, Jesus. He was dead to the
world and the body, his eyes and senses closed, his attention
withdrawn from them. And he hears the sweet Voice of
the Word emanating from the light form of Jesus and is
overwhelmed by his brightness. But Jesus holds him, meta-
phorically, by the hand: he raises him up out of the body,
appearing to Peter in a subtle form, a form suited to Peter's
inner advancement. And note, too, that this was all "Our
Lord, *willing* that I should behold his majesty" – the inner
Master is only met by *his* will, not by the will of the disciple.

Again, in a passage from one of the Nag Hammadi codices,
the light form of Jesus is described as appearing, "not in his
previous form", but like "a great angel of light". Perhaps,
then, one could also describe the astral form of a Master as
his "angelic form". Angels are beings of light, like all forms of
the astral or higher levels. They are seen inside and do not
appear in this world.

The Saviour appeared, not in his previous form,
But in the invisible spirit.
And his likeness resembles a great angel of light.

Sophia of Jesus Christ 91:10–13, NHL p. 222

6

RESURRECTION, GARMENTS
AND THE VOICE OF GOD

ESCAPE FROM EGYPT AND
THE SONG OF SWEETNESS

To one who is asleep while a fire ravages his house, nothing is more valuable than being awakened. To one who is held bondage in the tomb of the body, nothing is more liberating than escape from that body. To one for whom death is a passage which must one day be faced, nothing is more useful than an understanding of death. To one who wishes to be called from slumber, no sound is more compelling than the Voice of God.

Sentiments such as these have been expressed by all mystics throughout the ages, and in this chapter we seek out such expression in the apocryphal and gnostic literature, once again echoing the themes and images of *The Robe of Glory*.

The following is part of a long sequence of events, related in the *Assumption of the Virgin*, concerning the death of Jesus's mother, Mary. The happenings described in the *Assumption of the Virgin* are miraculous and marvellous in the extreme, and one is quite justified in dismissing their historical veracity. The interesting aspect, however, lies in the nature of the traditions and written sources used by this unknown writer of antiquity. For here, as in *The Robe of Glory*, we find again the imagery of a soul escaping from "Egypt", drawn on by a "Sweet Melody":

The Saviour spake, saying,
"Come thou most precious Pearl,
enter into the Treasury of Eternal Life." . . .

Thereafter, Peter lifted up the head of the body
and began to sing, saying:
"Israel is come out of Egypt." . . .

And the rest of the apostles sang
with exceedingly sweet voices, . . .
And an host of angels was . . .
sending forth a Song of Sweetness,
And the earth resounded
with the noise of that Great Melody.

Then the people came out of that city,
about fifteen thousand, and marvelled and said:
"What is this Sound of Great Sweetness?"

And there stood one and told them:
"Mary is gone out of the body,
and the disciples of Jesus
are singing praises about her." . . .

And the Lord spread forth his unstained hands
and received her holy and spotless soul.
and at the going forth of her spotless soul,
the place was filled with sweet odour
and light unspeakable,
And lo, a Voice from heaven was heard. . . .

And a great fragrance came from
that place . . . in paradise,
and a Melody of them that praised him
that was born of her:
And unto virgins only is it given to hear
that Sweet Melody wherewith
no man can be sated.

Assumption of the Virgin VII, XI, XII (Latin);
46, 49 (Greek) ANT p. 212, 213–214, 208–209

In this passage, the soul is first described as a precious pearl, capable of entering into the Treasury of Eternal Life.

Secondly, the writer uses the analogy of Israel's escape from Egypt as a description of Mary's leaving the body, putting the words into Peter's mouth. Here, Israel is used as a symbol for the soul and the metaphor seems to have been in common usage, perhaps even as a popular idiom. Like the pearl, it is certainly reminiscent of *The Robe of Glory*. We find it again in the *Exegesis on the Soul*, where the writer says that a Saviour only comes to one who — like the ancient children of Israel — sincerely yearns for release from the oppression and bondage of Egypt:

> Those who pray hypocritically deceive only themselves. Indeed, it is in order that He might know who is worthy of salvation that God examines the inward parts and searches the bottom of the heart. For no one is worthy of salvation who still loves the place of deception [this world, the place of illusion and impermanence]. . . .

> Certainly Israel would not have been visited in the first place, to be brought out of the land of Egypt, out of the house of bondage, if it had not sighed to God and wept for the oppression of its labours.

> *Exegesis on the Soul 136:21–27, 137:11–15,*
> *NHL p. 197, 198*

Thirdly, Mary's departure from the body is accompanied by the sound of the Song of Sweetness, which the writer puts into the mouths of Jesus's disciples, together with a host of angels flying in the sky. But from the strength of the imagery one gets the deep impression that the writer has read or heard, within his religious tradition, of the sweetness of the inner and heavenly music and though captivated enough by the idea to write it into his anecdote, he did not really understand what he had read or heard. In fact, in the full story, we also find the apostles being borne miraculously upon clouds or by the Holy Ghost, from wherever they were in the world, to be present at Mary's departure, while Jesus and Mary are borne upon clouds into Paradise, accompanied by angels.

It seems, therefore, that the writer has not understood the fact that God, Paradise, the Song of Sweetness and the place where souls go upon death are all inside us – not anywhere outside at all. Unless he has purposely chosen to speak allegorically and pseudo-historically to suit the social and religious exigencies of his time.

In the last two paragraphs, we also encounter "light unspeakable", a "sweet odour" and "great fragrance" – inner light and also a subtle and most sublime spiritual fragrance are characteristic of the Inner Melody. And, as is common in Biblical scenes, there is a voice from *heaven*, which is given *human* words to speak. If only the writers or their later editors had known the real nature of this Voice!

Finally, the writer adds, from his tradition or his sources, something which all mystics of the Divine Sound have pointed out: that only the pure and chaste can ever hear that Divine Music, which is so sweet, so captivating and so life-bestowing that no one can ever have enough.

With modern attitudes to the subject, this is worth a little consideration. To hear the Inner Music, the soul and mind must concentrate completely at the centre behind the eyes, and then be drawn out of the body by that Sound. Every ray of attention must be focused inside by a means taught at the time of initiation. The attention must become so concentrated within, that any input through the physical senses would fail to disturb the mind. The individual would not even notice it if someone hit his toes with a mallet or if an explosion took place down the street.

It takes years and years of dedicated meditation, blessed with the grace of a living Master, to develop this habit and trend of mind. And anything which takes the mind down into the body, away from the single eye, becomes a great hindrance to spiritual practice. The mind works by habit, and any downward flow sets up a tendency contrary to spiritual uplift. So indulgence in sex, with its intense focus of concentration upon almost the lowest level in the body, is rapidly discovered to be a great hindrance to resurrecting oneself from the body. Mystics, however, have said that to

avoid too much suppression one should allow the under-
standing to develop naturally, rather than by extreme force of
will. "It is better to marry than to burn," as St Paul wrote (1
Corinthians 7:9). Then a balance can be sought within
defined limits.

As one reads in the Acts of Paul or, as the same writing is
called in the Syriac, the History of Thecla:

> Ye have no resurrection otherwise,
> Except ye continue chaste,
> And defile not the flesh but keep it pure.

> *Acts of Paul II:12 (Greek), ANT p. 275*

> Ye cannot rise from the grave,
> Unless ye keep yourselves purely.

> *History of Thecla (Syriac), AAA p. 122*

THE TRUE RESURRECTION:
DIE THAT THOU MAYEST LIVE

The process by which the soul withdraws from the body and
ascends into the inner regions, is known as dying while living.
This is the true resurrection: the arising or awakening of the
soul from the deep slumber or death of physical life, whilst
still living in the tomb of the physical body. The topic was
discussed earlier (*see* pages 43–44 & 60–61) in the context of
the poem, but it is a subject of such importance that it deserves
further consideration here. And the following passages from
the apocryphal Acts demonstrate that the mystic view of
resurrection was common in early Christian times. Consider
the following, for example:

> We thy servants give thee thanks, O holy one,
> Who are assembled with good intent
> And are risen from death.

> *Acts of John 85, ANT p. 250*

And we will teach thee of that resurrection
Which he asserteth
That it is already come to pass . . .
We rise again [or, we have risen again]
When we have attained knowledge
    of the true God.

Acts of Paul II:14, ANT p. 275

Awake, thou also, and open thy soul.
Cast off the heavy sleep from thee.

Acts of John 21, ANT p. 230

Similarly, in the *Acts of Thomas*, Thomas speaks of Jesus as
the one who sleeps not, but awakens those who sleep; as the
one who truly lives, giving life to the dead people of this
world:

While ye sleep in this slumber
That weigheth down the sleepers,
He [Jesus], sleeping not, keepeth watch over you.

Acts of Thomas 66, ANT p. 395

To thee be glory, Living One
    who art from the Living One;
To thee be glory, Life-giver to many,
To thee be glory, defender and helper of them
    that come into thy refuge!
[Thou] that sleepest not,
    and awakest them that are asleep,
That livest and givest life to them that lie in death!

Acts of Thomas 60 (Greek and Syriac),
ANT p. 393, AAA p. 199

Identical and equally explicit sentiments are also expressed in
the writings of the Nag Hammadi library:

It is fitting that the soul regenerate herself and become again as she formerly was [becomes pure soul, attains Self-realization].

The soul then moves of her own accord [becomes a free soul], and – for her rejuvenation – she received the divine nature from the Father, so that she might be restored to the place where originally she had been.

> This is the resurrection from the dead.
> This is the ransom from captivity.
> This the upward journey of ascent to heaven.
> This is the way of ascent to the Father.

Exegesis on the Soul 134:6–15, NHL p. 196

The "regeneration of the soul" is its rebirth, its journey back to the Source of Life, its journey to Self-realization and God-realization. Then the soul becomes free from sin, free from birth and death, free from involvement with the Mind, realizing her unencumbered, natural state.

For this "rejuvenation", it is necessary that she receive mystic baptism in the Living Waters through the inward touch of a living Master. This is "receiving the divine nature of the Father", receiving the awakening touch of His essence, His Word.

And it entails "resurrection from the dead". It requires that the Master "ransom" the soul from the clutches of Satan – that the Master clean all the sins, karmas or impressions of past lives from the soul of his initiate in order that she be released from her "captivity" and slavery to Satan, the king of this world. The Master is the Merchant of God who buys or "ransoms" souls from Satan with the power and wealth of the Word. This is the road that ascends back to the Father.

In another treatise, the writer points out that once this purification has taken place:

We are drawn to heaven by him [the Saviour],
Like beams by the sun, not being restrained by anything.
This is the spiritual resurrection.

Treatise on the Resurrection 45:36–40, NHL p. 55

Regarding Jesus's resurrection, another – equally pithy – treatise points out that Jesus did not die and *then* resurrect (in his body). Rather he ascended to God or "rose up" *before* he died. Resurrection is release or ascension *from* the body, not *of* the body!

Those who say that the Lord died first
And then rose up are in error,
For he rose up first and then died.

Gospel of Philip 56:15–18, NHL p. 144

Similarly, the same author says that we too should learn to ascend or resurrect *before* we die so that we may find peace with God *after* "stripping off the flesh", or dying.

While we are in this world
It is fitting for us to acquire the resurrection,
So that when we strip off the flesh
We may be found in rest.

Gospel of Philip 66:16–19, NHL p. 149

And again, quite specifically, the writer of the *Testimony of Truth* asserts that there is no physical resurrection of the body on any "last day". People who believe such things, he says, are in error and do not know what they are talking about. They do not understand what God is, nor how He does things. And because of their confusion of mind, they do not even understand the scriptures to which they adhere. He says that those who have not been initiated into the living Word will die in the normal fashion and be born again in this world, adding that initiation is a rebirth.

Some say, "On the last day we will certainly arise in the resurrection." But they do not know what they are saying. . . . Do not expect, therefore, the carnal resurrection. . . .

They err in expecting a resurrection that is empty. They do not know the power of God, Nor do they understand the interpretation of the scriptures on account of their double-mindedness [confusion of thought]. Those who do not have the life-giving Word in their heart will die. . . .

We have been born again by the Word.

> *Testimony of Truth 34:25–27, 35:1–3, 29–30,*
> *37:3–9, 23–25, 40:5–6 NHL pp. 451–452*

Reading the lucid and outspoken style of *Exegesis on the Soul*, the *Treatise on the Resurrection* and the *Testimony of Truth* one wonders if perhaps they could all have been written by the same author. The mind behind all three is certainly similar. "We have been born again by the Word," says the latter writer. He, at least, seems to have been an initiate of a perfect Master.

One of the more well-known apocryphal writings, containing many mystical elements, is the *Acts of John*. There, as in the *Acts of Thomas*, one finds miraculous stories that in themselves are quite fantastic and impossible. Yet reading between the lines, one feels that many of these stories are a literalization of mystic allegory. Unless the author has purposely written allegory as pseudo-history, as a means of conveying spiritual truths.

In the story that follows, the line that first seems to have captivated the writer's imagination is, "Die that thou mayest live," and he repeats it twice. It is a statement reminiscent of St Paul's claim, "I die daily" (*1 Corinthians 15:31*). In his story, the writer tells the grisly tale of one Callimachus who is so enamoured of a young maiden, a disciple of the apostle John, that he even pursues her dead body to the graveyard to satisfy his desire. There, his grim intention is thwarted by a vision in which he is given the instruction: "Die that thou mayest live."

The main drift of the lost source of mystical teaching is clear. This world is a graveyard, where all souls are entombed in bodies. In order to live, the soul must pass through the experience of death in meditation, as we have previously described. This is what it means to die while living or to die a living death.

It is also possible that in the original parable the mind was symbolized as the restless young man in pursuit of a maiden. Endlessly he chases his desires, taking birth in the graveyard of this world. Here, in the realm of death, the objects of desire are all illusory or 'dead'. His desire is for the love of dead things. Perhaps, too, the maiden symbolized the pure soul, for all lower desire is really only a misdirection of the innate desire of the soul to return to its divine home. So the young man (the mind), unknowingly pursuing the maiden (seeking the purity of the soul), is misguided, and ends up in the graveyard (this world).

It is worth pointing out that in religious thought sin is made the object of moral criticism and its meaning is restricted only to certain 'sinful' acts and thoughts, becoming a source of confusion and guilt to many people. In the thinking of the mystics, however, sin is understood in a far wider context. Sin includes everything that binds a person to this world – good or bad. All the thoughts and actions of a lifetime, whatever their nature, leave their impressions upon the mind and result in further rebirth in this world. All of these impressions constitute sin. All attachments to this world, and all deeds – good or bad – which bring the soul back, are sins. This is a matter of fact, not a matter for guilt or moral judgement. And it means that every soul in this world is a 'sinner', that all souls are born along with their sins and because of their sins. So no one is in a position to point a finger at anyone else. One who is truly sinless does not come to this world at all, unless as a perfect Master.

In the story, I have taken some liberties in the first four lines in an attempt to restore the original allegory. The remainder reads like a mixture of a parable, a real event and a paeon of praise, all rolled into one, but it has been left as it is. How we

would have liked to see the sources of our writer: to have
looked over his shoulder as he wrote!

When my soul was stirred up [had risen up] . . .
And I had torn away the grave-clothes
   [of the body] . . .
And I had then come out of the grave
   [left the body] . . .
I saw a beautiful youth
   [met the light form of a Master] . . .
And from his eyes sparks of light came forth,
   and he uttered words to me, saying:
   "Callimachus, die that thou mayest live."

Now who he was, I knew not, O servant of God;
But now that thou hast appeared here;
   I recognize that he was an angel [messenger] of God,
   that I know well;
And this I know of a truth that God
   is proclaimed by thee,
   and of it I am persuaded.

Beseeching help therefore of thee,
   I take hold on thy feet.
I would become one of them that hope on Christ,
   that the voice may prove true which said to me,
   "Die that thou mayest live":

And that voice hath also fulfilled its effect,
   for he is dead – that faithless, disorderly,
   godless one [that I was] –
And I have been raised by thee,
   I who will be faithful, God-fearing,
   knowing the Truth,
   which I entreat thee may be shown me by thee."

And John, filled with great gladness
   and perceiving the whole spectacle
   of the salvation of man, said:

"What thy power is, Lord Jesu Christ, I know not,
    bewildered as I am at thy much compassion
    and boundless long-suffering.
O what a greatness that came down into bondage!
O unspeakable liberty brought into slavery by us!
O incomprehensible glory that is come unto us!

Thou that hast kept the dead tabernacle [body]
    safe from insult [sin];
That hast redeemed the man
    that stained himself with blood
    and chastened the soul of him
    that would defile the corruptible body;

Father that hast had pity and compassion
    on the man that cared not for thee;
We glorify thee, and praise and bless and
    thank thy great goodness and long-suffering. . . .

Glory be to our God, my child,
    who hath had mercy on thee,
    and made me worthy to glorify his power,
    and thee also by a good course to depart
    from thine abominable madness and drunkenness,
    and hath called thee unto his own rest
    and unto renewing of life."

Acts of John 76–78, ANT pp. 247–248

Taking the story at face value, John is overwhelmed at the
mercy and boundless grace of his Master. Engaged devotedly
in the service of his Master, he sees those who are deeply
bound up with the world, madly and drunkenly running
here and there, unaware that they are victims of their
own minds, being turned around and begging for initiation.
Yet there is no hint of moralizing in him; he is too steeped in
the compassion and love of his Master for that.

He observes how his Master is saving those souls who did
not even appear to want salvation, as well as those who had
been seekers of the Truth all their lives. He sees this show

going on and is amazed and filled with gratitude. He is aware
that for a soul that was running frantically after the world to
stop and turn in its tracks, subsequently devoting its energy
and mind to the Lord in meditation, is the greatest miracle of
all.

"What thy power is, Lord Jesu Christ," he exclaims, "I
know not." He has never seen such compassion, kindness and
tolerance. That such greatness – He who is one with God
– should come and dwell on earth, taking up the bondage of
human life, for our sakes! That one who has the freedom of
God should willingly be brought by us into apparent slavery!
That such incomprehensible glory should come to this world!
John's amazement and gratitude come to every disciple of a
living Master, though the people of the world cannot, in
general, understand it.

He sees how his Master Jesus has protected his disciple-to-
be from sin, forgiving him of other sins, cleansing him of the
effect of all his past actions and desires, that would otherwise
have kept him here for life after life. The apostle John, who
had perhaps been deputed to give the baptism instructions on
his Master's behalf, had had plenty of opportunity to see his
Master invisibly at work in the hearts of his marked sheep,
making his chosen souls worthy and capable of loving him,
giving them inner peace and filling them with the riches of the
inner life. There are times when John, quite naturally, is
overwhelmed.

The *Acts of John* contains many such beautiful passages,
full with the vibrancy of personal experience. Somewhere, not
far behind the confusion of its content, lay the living expe-
rience of disciple and Master.

GARMENTS OF THE SOUL

Garments and robes have been common mystic symbols
throughout the ages and the gnostic writings were no
exception to their use. As in *The Robe of Glory* or in Jesus's
parable of the wedding feast, garments may refer to the true
nature of the soul: its garment or quality of light, its innate
and well-fitting garment of love and mystic self-knowledge.

Alternatively, garments are a way of describing the coverings of the soul in the Mind regions – the causal, astral, and physical bodies.

In the *Gospel of Philip*, in a neat play on words, the author uses the metaphor in both ways, pointing out that, in the physical realm, man is more than the clothes he wears and is more than the body with which he has been covered. But in the higher realms the 'garment' of light and love is the true nature of the soul, comprising its essence.

> In this world, those who put on garments
> Are better than the garments.
> In the kingdom of heaven,
> The garments are better than those
> Who have put them on.
>
> *Gospel of Philip 57:19–22, NHL p. 144*

And echoing the parable of Jesus and *The Robe of Glory*, the same writer says that no one can "go in to the King", can merge into God, without his royal robe:

> No one will be able to go in to the King if he is naked.
>
> *Gospel of Philip 58:15–17, NHL p. 145*

Similarly, in *Allogenes*, the soul describes being taken out of the garment of the physical body to a realm beyond description:

> I was taken by the Eternal Light
> Out of the garment that was upon me,
> And taken up to a holy place
> Whose likeness cannot be revealed in the world.
>
> *Allogenes 58:27–33, NHL p. 496*

Likewise, the *Teachings of Silvanus* refer to the power of

sexual desire to keep the soul in bondage to the bodily
garment. This he calls the "garment of fornication" since
only the physical garment is reproduced by means of sex.
The author exhorts the soul to abandon all desire for the
physical form and to find the true, pure and radiant self
within:

O my son,
Strip off the old garment of fornication,
And put on the garment which is clean and shining,
That you may be beautiful in it.
But when you have this garment, protect it well.

Release yourself from every bond
So that you may acquire freedom.
If you cast out of yourself this desire
Whose devices are many,
You will release yourself from the sins of lust.

Teachings of Silvanus 105:13–25, NHL p. 389

And referring directly to the Word – to Wisdom – he
describes it as a "shining robe", also pointing out that Christ
is one with the Word, with Wisdom. He is the straight path
on which to travel in order to put on the shining and mystic
robe.

He [Christ] is Wisdom; he is also the Word.
He is the Life, the Power, and the Door.
He is the Light, the Angel, and the Good Shepherd. . . .

Knock within yourself as upon a door,
And walk within yourself as on a straight road.
For if you walk on the road,
It is impossible for you to go astray.
And if you knock with Wisdom,
You knock on hidden treasures.

For since he [Christ] is Wisdom,
He makes the foolish man wise.
Wisdom is a holy kingdom and a shining robe.

Teachings of Silvanus 106:23–28, 31–35,
107:1–6, NHL p. 390

In the *Trimorphic Protennoia*, the author – following a literary style of the times – writes in the name of the Father. The soul is invited into the presence of God where it will receive its royal robes and "become gloriously glorious". In the poem, the "Baptists" are those who give baptism – the perfect Masters. Then the soul will shine with the light and glory it possessed when it first left the Father. Likewise, "those who give glory", those who "enthrone", and "those who give robes" are all references to the perfect Masters.

I am inviting you into the exalted, perfect Light.
Moreover, as for this Light, when you enter it
You will be glorified by those who give glory,
And those who enthrone will enthrone you.
You will accept robes from those who give robes
And the Baptists will baptize you
And you will become gloriously glorious,
The way you first were when you were Light.

Trimorphic Protennoia 45:12–20, NHL p. 519

In the *Paraphrase of Shem*, it is the Father who puts on His royal garment when He emanates Himself as the Word:

I put on my garment
    which is the garment of the light of the Majesty –
    which I am.
I came in the appearance of the Spirit
    to consider the whole [one] light
    which was in the depths of the Darkness.

Paraphrase of Shem 8:33–36, 9:1–3, NHL p. 345

The Father comes as the Spirit, the Word, to the creation. He "considers the whole light which was in the depths of Darkness" – He sees Himself in everything, even in the apparent darkness of His creation.

The writer then speaks of the Son of God, the "Son of the Majesty", who comes from the Divine Infinite Thought, the primal emanation or Word of God, as a Saviour or Master.

> My likeness, the Son of the Majesty,
> Is from my infinite Thought [Essence],
> Since I am for him a universal likeness
> Which does not lie, [which is above illusion]. . . .
>
> His appearance is in my beautiful garment of light
> Which is the Voice of the immeasurable Thought.
>
> *Paraphrase of Shem 12:1–5, 7–9, NHL p. 346*

He says that the Son is of the image or likeness of God, which is above all unreality, above all illusion. Though the Son is a manifestation or "appearance" of the Infinite, he remains merged into the Lord's "beautiful garment of Light" and the "Voice" of the highest essence.

The use of the term "Thought" should not be confused with our definitions of Mind. The Coptic, Greek and Semitic languages of those times abounded in a wealth of mystic terms which become difficult for scholars to translate into our English language. In this context, Thought means the essence of being. Just as human beings without thought have no life, similarly without the 'Divine Thought' there is no creation. But God does not 'think' as we do! Its use here is as a metaphor.

The author then points out our inherent unity with the Source, the "single sole Light which came into being". And that by its own Will, the same Light then came as the Word, without its "Universal garment", to raise us from our human condition in this world, this "feeble Nature".

> We are that single sole Light which came into being.
> He appeared in another root in order
> That the power of the Spirit

Might be raised from the feeble Nature.
For by the will of the great Light,
I came forth from the exalted Spirit . . .
Without my Universal garment.

Paraphrase of Shem 12:10–19, NHL p. 346

The descent of the Son and Saviour is then charted as he
moves out from the Lord. First, the "garment of Light", the
royal robe, is replaced with a "garment of fire" acquired in the
"Middle Region". From this and other gnostic texts it is clear
that the "Middle Region", sometimes translated as the Midst,
refers to what we have termed the realms of the Mind.

Then, by the will of the Majesty,
I took off my garment of Light.
I put on another garment of fire which has no form,
[And] which is from the mind of the power
     which was separated,
And which was prepared for me, according to my will,
     in the Middle Region.
For the Middle Region covered it with a dark power
In order that I might come and put it on.

[Thence] I went down to Chaos
To save the whole [one] light from it.

Paraphrase of Shem 18:1–15, NHL p. 349

The "garment of fire", therefore, refers to the sparkling astral
form or covering, or perhaps to the causal body – or maybe
to both. The Middle Region, where separation takes place,
which is the source of "a dark power" and where the "garment
of fire" is handed out by the "mind of the power which was
separated", clearly refers to the realms of the Universal Mind
where the soul is clothed in the various bodies, becoming
deeply separated from God.

    In the poet's account, the Saviour then descends to Chaos,
an apt term used for the labyrinth or general mayhem of this
physical world, "to save the whole [one] light" from the "dark

power" (Satan). This, of course, is the same story we have encountered so many times before.

Picking up the same story from the *Dialogue of the Saviour*, the Saviour or the Son of Man greets the souls in the physical universe:

> And the Son of Man greeted them and said to them,
>   "A seed from a power [the soul] was deficient
>   and it went down to the abyss of the earth.
>
> And the Greatness remembered it
>   and He sent the Word to it.
> [And] It [the Word] brought it up
>   into His presence. . . ."
>
> Then said he to his disciples,
>   "Have I not told you that by a Visible Voice
>   and a flash of lightning
>   will the good be taken up to the Light." . . .
>
> As they stood there, he saw two spirits
>   bringing a single soul with them
>   in a great flash of lightning.
> And a word came forth from the Son of Man,
>   saying, "Give them their garment!"
> And the small one [the soul]
>   became like the big one [the Word, the Saviour].
>
> *Dialogue of the Saviour 135:17–22, 136:5–10, 17–22,*
> *NHL pp. 250–251*

THE VOICE AND THE SON

As must have become very clear, no factor is more central to the teachings of a perfect Master than that of the Word. And most particularly, that this Word can be both heard and seen. It is both Divine Music and Divine Light. Hearing and seeing are the two "guides" of the soul in the inner realms, just as light and sound are so important to us in this world.

It is for this reason that in the gnostic and apocryphal writings, the inner music of the Word has commonly been called the Voice of God, the Silent Voice, the Visible Voice, the Voice of Truth, the Real Voice, the Ineffable Voice, the Unreproducible Voice, the Hidden Voice or, simply, the Voice. It is also called the Name of God, the Thought of God, the Nous, the Logos, the Hidden Wisdom, the Immeasurable Spring, the Radiant Waters, the Living Waters, the Comforter and by many other names.

For a man who has fallen into a deep, dark well, nothing is of more importance than the light at the top, the sound of his friend's voice outside, and the rope let down by his friend. To souls who realize that they are lost in the darkness of this world, nothing is of more value than personal living contact with a Friend of God. And the rope he passes down to the one in the well is the Word, the Visible Voice of God. The following passages amply demonstrate this mystic fact.

In the *Acts of Thomas*, the Voice is called the Comforter, the "port and harbour" or safe haven of those who travel through the inner realms. In a song of praise and gratitude to his Master Jesus, Thomas says:

O Companion and ally of the feeble;
Hope and confidence of the poor [in spirit];
Refuge and lodging of the weary;
Voice that came forth from on high,
    Comforter dwelling within the hearts of thy believers
    port and harbour of them
    that pass through the regions of the rulers:
Physician that healest without payment. . . .

Thou didst descend into Sheol [this world]
    with mighty power,
    and the dead saw thee and became alive. . . .
Thou didst ascend with great glory,
    and didst take up with thee
    all who sought refuge with thee,
    and in thy footsteps, all thy redeemed followed;

and thou didst bring them into thy fold,
And didst join them with thy sheep:

Son of perfect mercy, the Son that for the love of man
  who wast sent unto us with power
From the Supreme and Perfect Country
  [from the Land of the Father, from God];
Lord of [spiritual] possessions that cannot be defiled;
Wealthy [One], who hast filled thy creation
  with the treasure of thy wealth . . .
[Thou] that servest thy servants
  that they may live; . . .
That satisfiest our thirsty souls
  with thine own good things: . . .

Be unto them a guide in the land of error:
Be unto them a physician in the land of sickness:
Be unto them a rest in the land of the weary:
  make them pure in a polluted land,
Be their physician both of bodies and souls:
  make them holy shrines and temples of thee,
  and let thy Holy Spirit dwell in them.

> *Acts of Thomas 156 (Greek and Syriac),*
> *ANT pp. 432–433, AAA pp. 288–289*

For his disciples, Jesus was the companion, the ally, the refuge and the lodging. He is equated with the Voice, the Word of God. He was sent by God to collect certain sheep or souls from the hell of this world, the land of error and sickness; to carry them up with him, back to God, to guide and help them to live in this world; to purify their minds of all traces of past sin; to satisfy their spiritual thirst with the Living Waters of the Word and to make them true temples or shrines of the Living God.

  In a similar passage, we read:

Our Lord – Companion of his servants,
  and guide and conductor of those who believe in Him,
  and refuge and repose of the afflicted,

and hope of the poor, and deliverer of the feeble,
and healer of sick souls, life-giver of the universe,
and Saviour of all creatures. . . .

Thou art the discloser of hidden secrets,
and the revealer of mysterious sayings. . . .

Thou didst hurl the Evil One [Satan, Universal Mind]
from his power,
and didst call with thy Voice to the dead,
and they became alive. . . .

Thou wast the Ambassador,
and wast sent from the supernal heights,
because thou art able to do the living
and perfect will of thy Sender.

Acts of Thomas (Syriac), AAA pp. 153–154

Again in the *Acts of Thomas*, the Voice is explicitly stated not
to belong "to the nature of this bodily organ", that the Voice
is in no way similar to a physical voice. In this excerpt, a
young man is talking to the apostle Thomas:

I have found him that showeth me fair things,
that I may take hold on them [experience them],
even the Son of Truth,   ·
who scattereth away the mist
and enlighteneth his own creation. . . .

But I beseech thee, O man of God,
cause me to behold him again,
and to see him that is now hidden from me,
that I may hear his Voice
whereof I am not able to express the wonder,
for it belongeth not to the nature
of this bodily organ.

Acts of Thomas 34, ANT p. 381

In the Syriac version, the same passage reads:

> I beg of thee, apostle of God,
>   sow in me thy Word of Life,
>   so that I may again hear perfectly the Voice of him
>   who delivered me unto thee and said to thee:
> "This is one of those who shall live through thee,
>   and henceforth let him be with thee."

Acts of Thomas (Syriac), AAA p. 176

In this case, the meaning is true, mystically, whichever version one reads, leaving one to muse upon which is the more original version. For even if the *Acts of Thomas* was originally written in Syriac, it is likely to have been edited by a later hand, while the Greek translation we have could have been made from an earlier Syriac edition. Or perhaps the author wrote both the Syriac and the Greek versions and thus felt quite at liberty to add variations on his own theme. This would certainly explain why both versions express similar, yet different, mystical truths.

Just as the inner Voice is not heard with "this bodily organ", similarly, the light form of a Master is not seen with the physical eyes, but by the "eyes of the mind", that is, by the inner eye or inner faculty of sight. In the anecdote from which the following excerpt is drawn, Thomas is in conversation with a captain in the service of a certain King Mazdai:

> And the captain said: "Show me him [Jesus],
>   that I may entreat him and believe in him."

> And the apostle said:
> "He appeareth not unto these bodily eyes,
>   but is found by the eyes of the mind."

Acts of Thomas 65, ANT p. 395

Here, the corresponding translation from the Syriac reads:

The apostle saith to him: "As far as thou art able,
    stretch thy mind upward,
    because he is not visible now to these bodily eyes."

Acts of Thomas (Syriac), AAA p. 203

This supplies a further shade of meaning, for it is true that in
order to awaken the "eyes of the mind" one has to ascend
within oneself, "to stretch thy mind upward".

Later, when the same king, impressed by Thomas's aura of
genuine spirituality, asks to be told the name of his Master,
Thomas replies obliquely:

Thou canst not hear his True Name at this time:
But the name that was given unto him is Jesus Christ.

Acts of Thomas 163, ANT p. 435

It means that the true Name of God is the Word, the Voice,
and that the true form of the Master is this Name or Word,
a Name that cannot be heard with the physical ears or uttered
with the physical mouth.

A VOICE SPEAKING SOFTLY

In the short Nag Hammadi tractate, the *Thought of Norea*,
one finds a prayer and invocation to:

Father of All, Ennoia [Thought] of the Light
Dwelling in the heights,
Above the regions below, Light dwelling in the heights,
Voice of Truth, upright Nous, untouchable Logos,
And ineffable Voice, incomprehensible Father!

Thought of Norea 27:11–20, NHL p. 446

Here, as in the ensuing passages, the All refers to the creation
with all its host of higher realms and sub-powers. In these
ringing passages from *Trimorphic Protennoia*, so reminiscent

in style of a similar passage from the tenth chapter of the Hindu *Bhagavad Gita*, it is the Supreme Lord who is 'speaking':

I am the Invisible One within the All. . . .
I am immeasurable, ineffable, yet whenever I wish,
I shall reveal myself of my own accord.
I am the head of the All.
I exist before the All, and I am the All,
Since I exist in everyone.

I am a Voice speaking softly.
I exist from the first.
I dwell within the Silence. . . .
And it is the hidden Voice that dwells within me,
Within the incomprehensible, immeasurable Thought,
Within the immeasurable Silence.

I descended to the midst of the underworld [this world]
And I shone down upon the darkness.
It is I who poured forth the water.
It is I who am hidden within Radiant Waters.
I am the one who gradually put forth [manifested,
    emanated] the All by my Thought.
It is I who am laden with the Voice.
It is through me that Gnosis comes forth. . . .
I am perception [enlightenment] and knowledge,
Uttering a Voice by means of Thought.

I am the real Voice. I cry out in everyone,
And they recognize it [the Voice],
Since a seed [of me] dwells in [each of] them.
I am the Thought of the Father
And through me proceeded the Voice,
That is, the knowledge of everlasting things. . . .

I revealed myself . . . among those who recognize me.
For it is I who am joined [who am within] everyone
By virtue of the . . . exalted Voice,
Even a Voice from the Invisible Thought.

And it is Immeasurable,
Since it dwells in the Immeasurable One. . . .
It is a Light dwelling in Light. . . .

It is we, [separate and alone in the visible world,
Who] are saved by the hidden Wisdom,
By means of the ineffable, immeasurable Voice.
And that which is hidden within us [the soul]
Pays the tributes of his fruit to the Water of Life.

Then the Son who is perfect in every respect –
That is, the Word who originated through that Voice;
Who proceeded from the height;
Who has within him the Name; who is a Light –
He [the Son] revealed the everlasting things
And all the unknowns were known.

And those things difficult to interpret and secret,
He revealed,
And as for those who dwell in Silence
   with the First Thought,
He taught of them.
And he revealed himself to those
Who dwell in darkness,
And he showed himself to those
Who dwell in the abyss,
And to those who dwell in the hidden treasuries
He told ineffable mysteries,
And he taught unrepeatable doctrines to all those
Who became Sons of the Light.

> *Trimorphic Protennoia 35:24, 27–35, 36:1–10,*
> *12–19, 22–28, 32–36, 37:1–20 NHL pp. 513–514*

And I hid myself in everyone
And revealed myself within them,
And every mind [and soul] seeking me longed for me,
For it is I who gave shape to the All
When it had no form.
And I transformed their forms into other forms
   [reincarnation] . . .

It is through me that the Voice originated
And it is I who put the breath [of life, initiation]
    within my own [chosen ones].
And I cast into them the eternally Holy Spirit
And I ascended and entered my Light. . . .

I am the Word who dwells in the ineffable Voice.
I dwell in undefiled Light. . . .
The Word is a hidden Light, bearing a Fruit of Life,
Pouring forth a Living Water
From the invisible, unpolluted, immeasurable Spring,
That is the unreproducible Voice.

Trimorphic Protennoia 45:21–31, 46:5–6,
16–20, NHL p. 519

7

THE PARABLE OF THE PEARL MERCHANT

A LOST PARABLE OF JESUS?

In a short tractate from the Nag Hammadi library, the *Acts of Peter and the Twelve Apostles*, there are the traces of a beautiful parable, perhaps one told by Jesus himself, though it is somewhat more elaborate than his usual style. Set into a pseudo-historical framework, with Peter, the apostles, some beggars and a mysterious pearl merchant as the central characters, it is clear that the short text covering only five pages in translation is a composite made up from a number of sources. Douglas Parrott, one of the two translators, points out the awkward links between the sections, inconsistencies in the flow of the story, shifts from first person to third person narrative and so on. He suggests that the Coptic version we have has been compiled from four independent sources, indicating that it was probably a well-loved tale, often repeated in various guises, as is the way with stories. It is also possible that the anecdote was told as a pseudo-historical allegory, much like other apocryphal Acts.

The mystic meaning of the story, however, is clear enough, and in the following rendering I have attempted to restore something of the original, using as much of the existing text as possible, though I doubt very much if I have reconstructed it correctly. The main change has been to remove Peter and the apostles as its central characters, replacing them with a group of travellers. Most of the rest remains the same.

THE PEARL MERCHANT
AND HIS CITY OF NINE GATES

The beginning of the original story is missing and we pick it
up where the party, having set out on a journey and taken ship
at "an opportune moment, which came to us from the Lord",
are brought "to a small city in the midst of the sea". It is, one
presumes, an island, though later in the story they travel
overland to another city. This is just one of the existing
parable's inconsistencies. The story is related in the first
person, where the 'I' is the leader of the group.

And when I enquired about the name of this city from
residents who were standing on the dock, a man among
them answered, saying, "The name of this city is
Habitation, a place of endurance. We inhabit here
because we endure."

I responded, saying, "Justly have men called it so
because cities are entirely inhabited by those who endure
trials, difficulties and storms. But a precious kingdom
arises out of their endurance. For the city of every person
who takes upon himself the yoke of God will be included
in the kingdom of heaven."

Then, after we had gone ashore with the baggage, I
went into the city to seek advice about lodging. And a
man came out wearing a cloth bound around his waist,
girded with a gold belt. Also a shawl was tied over his
chest, extending over his shoulders and covering his head
and his hands.

I gazed at the man, because his appearance and
bearing were so beautiful. There were four parts of his
body that I could see: the soles of his feet and a part of
his chest and the palms of his hands and his face. These
things I was able to see. A book cover was in his left
hand. A staff of styrax wood was in his right hand. And
his voice was resounding as he slowly spoke, crying out
in the city, "Pearls! Pearls!"

Thinking him to be a man of that city, I began to speak
with him and said, "My brother and my friend . . . !"

But he interrupted me immediately, saying, "Rightly

did you say, 'My brother and my friend.' What is it that you seek from me?"

I said to him, "I ask you about lodging for myself and my companions also, because we are strangers here."

He said to me, "For this reason have I myself just said, 'My brother and my friend,' because I am also a fellow stranger like you."

Having said these things, he began again to cry out, "Pearls! Pearls!" At this, the rich men of the city heard his voice. They came out of their hidden storerooms. And some were looking out from the storerooms of their houses. Others looked out from their upper windows. But they did not see that they could gain anything from him, because there was no pouch on his back nor bundle inside his cloth and shawl. And because of their disdain they did not even acknowledge him.

He, for his part, did not reveal himself to them. They returned to their storerooms, saying, "This man is mocking us."

But the poor of that city heard his voice, and they came to the seller of pearls, saying, "Please take the trouble to show us the pearl so that we may at least see it with our own eyes. For we are poor. And we do not have the kind of price required to pay for one. But only show us a pearl that we might say to our friends that we have seen a pearl with our own eyes."

He answered, saying to them, "If it is possible, come to my city, so that I may not only display it before your very eyes, but also give you one for nothing."

And they, the poor of that city, when they heard this, said, "We are beggars and we know for sure that a man does not give a pearl to a beggar. It is bread and money that are usually received. So now the kindness which we want to receive from you is that you show us the pearl, before our eyes – because such pearls are not to be found amongst the poor, especially amongst beggars such as us."

But he answered and said to them, "If it is possible, you yourselves come to my city, so that I may not only show it to you, but give it to you for nothing." And the poor and the beggars rejoiced because of the man who gives away his wealth for nothing.

I then came forward and said to the one selling pearls, "I would like to know your name and details of the way to your city."

He answered and said, "If you seek my name, Lithargoel is my name, the interpretation of which is 'a lightweight, gazelle-like stone'.

"And concerning the road to the city, about which you asked, I will tell you of it. No man is able to go on that road, except one who has forsaken everything that he has. For many are the robbers and wild beasts on that road. The one who carries bread with him on the road, the black dogs will kill because of the bread. The one who carries a costly garment of the world with him, the robbers kill because of the garment. The one who carries water with him, the wolves kill because of the water, since they are thirsty for it. The one who is anxious about meat and green vegetables, the lions eat because of the meat. And if he evades the lions, the bulls will devour him because of the green vegetables."

When he had said these things, the people sighed, saying within themselves, "Great hardships lie on this road! Only a Friend of God can give us the power to walk upon it!"

And he, hearing our sighs and seeing the sadness on our faces, said to us, "Why do you sigh, if you already know where to seek for help? Such a Friend is a great power for giving strength, for it is the Father who has sent him."

Then I asked him, "What is the name of the place to which you go, your city?"

He replied, "This is the name of my city: *Nine Gates*. And let us praise God that we are mindful that the tenth gate lies in the head."

And after this we went away from him in peace and set out upon the road to the city that he, Lithargoel, had appointed for us. In a bond of faith we forsook everything as he had told us to do. We evaded the black dogs because they found no bread on us [no attachments to worldly things]. We evaded the robbers because they did not find [the desire for] costly garments on us. We evaded the wolves because they did not find the water with us for which they thirsted [they did not find us thirsty for the water for which they thirsted]. We evaded the lions, because they did not find the desire for meat in us. We evaded the bulls because they did not find green vegetables.

And so we reached the city. And there, resting in front of the city gate [singular], a great joy came upon us and a peaceful carefreeness. And we talked with each other about those matters which are not distractions of this world. Rather, we spoke about the things of God and of Lithargoel.

And as we spoke, Lithargoel, having changed, came out to greet us. He had taken on the appearance of a physician, since an unguent box was under his arm, and a young disciple was following him carrying a pouch full of medicine. But we did not recognize him.

But I responded and said to him, "We want you to do us a favour, because we are strangers, and take us to the house of Lithargoel before evening comes."

He said, "Out of the goodness of my heart I will show it to you. But I am amazed at how you knew this good man. For he does not reveal himself to every man, since he himself is the son of a great king. But rest yourselves a little, while I go to attend one who is sick. Then I will return." And he hurried away and soon returned.

And on his return, as we looked at him, he loosened the garment which clothed him – the one in which he had concealed himself because of us – revealing to us who in truth he really was.

Acts of Peter and the Twelve Apostles 1–9,
NHL pp. 289–293

Whether or not this gentle reconstruction is fair to the lost original, certain mystical points still remain valid. The city called "Habitation", set like an island in the midst of the sea, is the physical body, existing like an island in the midst of the stormy ocean of the world. The soul is an island because we are isolated from each other by our minds and bodies. It is called "Habitation" because a habitation is only a temporary dwelling, not a permanent abode. The soul takes birth in a physical body, but does not remain here forever.

Moreover, physical life is nothing but endurance. And no greater endurance and effort are required than upon the journey to fulfil life's greatest purpose. But if we set out, then we ultimately achieve that goal, we are "included in the kingdom of heaven" – we find God within ourselves.

The travellers are strangers in that city, just as the soul encumbered with mind and matter is a stranger living in this world. It is a prince living as a pauper. It is the son of a king who has fallen asleep in Egypt, becoming the slave of a foreign ruler. The travellers coming to a city called "Habitation" are therefore the souls, taking birth in physical bodies. And here, due to the difficulties of existence and their apparent divorce from God, the souls are tired and weary.

The traveller therefore goes in search of rest and lodging and on his way he meets a man of most beautiful face and bearing, but he does not know who the man is, taking him only for another resident of that city. The man, however, points out that he, too, is a fellow stranger, agreeing that he is indeed a "friend and brother".

This is the role of the Master, who approaches his fellow human beings as a friend and brother, a fellow traveller and stranger in this world. By being human, he is able to win their trust, their confidence and their love. A Master is also of beautiful face and bearing.

The man then reveals himself as a pearl bearer, calling out, "Pearls! Pearls!" The "rich" people make the automatic assumption that he must be *selling* pearls, and taking one look at his appearance, they decide that he cannot possibly possess the goods that he is proclaiming, anyway. So they return to their storehouse of worldly affairs. Because of their own bent of mind, they never imagine that he might not be selling the pearls at all. They unthinkingly impute to him the same greed and self-interest by which they themselves are motivated.

The Masters come to this world and give their message. They offer the pearls of spiritual wisdom and mystical experience. But the "rich" "disdain even to acknowledge him." With little more than a passing glance, they write him off as having nothing that they want. The "rich people" signify those who are attached to the riches of the world, to the worldly 'treasure', to worldly affairs – it does not just mean the wealthy. It refers to those who are constantly absorbed in the play of physical life, never giving a thought to any higher purpose. It is a question of one's mental attachment and attitude, not necessarily of one's material possessions. In fact, rich people may sometimes be less attached to the world than poor people.

So the people of the world reject the teachings of the Masters. But the real spiritual seekers, on the other hand, the more humble ones – the "poor people" and the "beggars" – are so aware of their human inadequacies that they cannot at first consider that they would ever be given such wealth.

In reality, almost everyone in this world, though potentially spiritually rich, is actually a beggar. A beggar can only beg. He is entirely reliant upon the goodwill and favour of benefactors. Similarly, although the soul is of royal blood, it is so encumbered in this world with its tawdry collection of baggages from past lives, that it needs to be *given* the gift of spiritual wealth. Sooner or later, real seekers become aware of this, that they are like beggars, that their efforts towards the spiritual heights, without some higher blessing, only lead them round in circles. And only one who realizes his condition as a beggar will beg.

So in the story, when offered a pearl, only the beggars and the poor people, those who know that spiritually they are paupers and destitute, ask to see a pearl, just to catch a glimpse of one.

But the good-hearted pearl merchant informs them that actually he has come to *give* them each a pearl. They will not have to pay a penny. This is a characteristic of a perfect Master, that he never takes anything from his disciples. He lives off his own income, teaching his disciples to do likewise, yet spending his entire life in their service.

The pearl merchant, however, does make one stipulation before this treasure can be received: they must all leave their own city and come to his city.

The "poor people" are grateful when they realize this simple yet amazing fact, that the wealth of the spiritual pearl will be given to them, absolutely free of charge. The narrator then comes forward and asks two pertinent questions: firstly, "Who are you? – What is your name?" and secondly, "How do we get to your city?"

Naturally, when a person is made such a generous offer, he questions the motives of the one making the offer. At best, they think that the individual must simply be a crank or a misguided enthusiast. A Master teaches with such confidence that those who hear him are impressed. Yet he seems to have no axe to grind and nothing personal to achieve. As a human being, they can see that he is certainly a balanced and wise person. He has a wonderful sense of humour and is very kind and affectionate. He advocates no extreme measures or ascetic practices. He does not even claim to be a Master, but refers all credit to his own Master. He is never arrogant or overbearing, or filled with self-importance.

Yet he talks of such high matters, though without any fanatical tendency or any attempt to proselytize. He gives no allegiance to any religion in particular but only points out the spiritual truths which lie at the base of all religions. He never creates divisions, but only tries to unite people on the common platform of love and universal spirituality. He also seems to be fully in control of himself and to know exactly what he is doing. So naturally people want to know who he is, where he comes from and "By what authority doest thou these things?" (*St Matthew 21:23*).

The pearl merchant replies that his name is Lithargoel, meaning a lightweight stone with a gleam like that of a gazelle's eye – a pearl. His name, then, is Pearl, and referring back to the quotations from the *Acts of John* and the *Acts of Peter* (pages 31–32), we can see that in the time of Jesus, the Master was referred to as the "True Pearl Ineffable". So Lithargoel is the Master, the Word made flesh. But being cloaked and concealed in a human form, no one as yet recognizes him for who he really is.

Lithargoel then describes to the seekers who are gathered around him the nature of the path they must travel to reach his city. In essence, he tells them that they must detach themselves from the world. He is describing the inner path to them. They can take no worldly cares or possessions with them upon the journey, he says. But this is the only price that they must pay in order to receive the pearl. Certainly, Lithargoel is not the usual kind of merchant!

The mind goes and stays wherever its thoughts, desires and attractions are. So, while still living in the world and discharging all obligations, a Master teaches that one must *mentally* and inwardly become detached from everything – to live in the world but to be inwardly free of it. "Unless ye fast from the world, ye shall in no wise find the kingdom of God," Jesus says, in the *Gospel of Thomas* (*SOL p. 19*). But the "fasting" is inward. Simply rejecting the world does not necessarily prevent one from thinking about it. Through suppression, it may even have a reverse effect.

This is the meaning of the various examples given. The "robbers and wild beasts" are relatives, friends and associates who absorb all of an individual's attention, successfully waylaying their mind on the road to the meeting with the inner Master.

They are also the human weaknesses that everyone carries with them. These are the real culprits, waylaying the mind and soul on their inner ascent, for without these weaknesses, the outer "robbers and wild beasts" can take no hold upon a person.

At this, the people sigh. Echoing the astonishment of Jesus's disciples after he had advised the young man to give up all he had, they ask, "Who then can be saved?" (*St Matthew 19:25*). And, in the words of John the Baptist, the reply is: "A man can receive nothing, except it be *given* him from heaven" (*St John 3:27*). And the way this gift is given by God is through one who comes from the kingdom of Heaven: the Master must *give* the pearl to a beggar.

The traveller then asks Lithargoel, "What is the name of the place to which you go, your city?"

And he replies, "This is the name of my city: *Nine Gates*.

And let us praise God that we are mindful that the tenth gate lies in the head."

This reply alone alerts us to the mystic nature of the parable, for many mystics have called the human body, "the house of nine gates" or "the city of nine gates". Considered simply, we can see that the body has nine openings through which the attention spreads into the world of the physical senses. They are the two eyes, two ears, two nostrils, the mouth and the two lower openings. In meditation, an initiate is taught to withdraw all the attention from these nine gates and to focus it at a tenth gate. And where is this tenth gate? It "lies in the head". This single eye or door of the house which opens inwards lies behind and slightly above the two physical eyes, though it is entirely subtle in nature, having no physical organ or counterpart. It is an "eye of the mind". This is the door at which Jesus said:

> Ask, and it shall be given you;
> Seek and ye shall find;
> Knock and it shall be opened unto you.
>
> *St Matthew 7:7*

When the soul and mind focus at this point, the attention is completely withdrawn from the nine gates and concentrates at this tenth gate in the head. When the practitioner is successful in meditation, the body below the eyes becomes absolutely numb and devoid of sensation. This is the process of death, though it is experienced in full consciousness, under full control and with great joy.

The soul and mind then pass out of the body, through this tenth gate. They go inside and there, on the threshold of the inner mansions, they meet the radiant or light form of the Master. They have come to the "city" of the Master.

In a world where death is a certain reality which all must face, this understanding and personal experience of the nature of death is one of the greatest gifts conferred by a Master upon a disciple. "Let us praise God that we are mindful" of it, says Lithargoel. Such knowledge is a rare possession in this world.

Continuing the narrative, the travellers then set out upon the journey to the inner city, avoiding the "robbers" and "wild beasts" along the way. They keep their minds concentrated and out of all entanglement with the world. Otherwise, if one thought of the world disturbs the peace and concentration of the mind, the mind leaves the tenth gate and runs out into the world: then the practitioner has been "robbed" or attacked by "wild beasts", and has to regather his concentration once again.

Here we can see why it is the "desire" for costly garments and the things of the world which waylay a soul on its journey to the inner citadel. For in meditation the body is not active, only the mind. There is nothing physical about the journey to the inner city of the Master, to the inner realms where the light form of the Master is encountered. It is travelled entirely on the road of longing and spiritual yearning. It is this that detaches the mind and takes it inside. Disturbances to the mind, arising from the desire for worldly things and activities, bring the mind back into the world. Hence, Lithargoel is perfectly correct: all desires of the world have to be relinquished in order that his inner city may be reached.

Travelling by way of meditation, then, the group of poor and humble beggars, devoid of all mental worldliness, come to Lithargoel's city, and there, sitting before the gate, which – significantly – is singular, they find themselves in a state of great peace and bliss. This is the condition which the disciple experiences whilst 'sitting' at the tenth gate, the single eye, in meditation. In a state of great peace, bliss, love and longing, he awaits the coming of his Master, for the tenth gate is opened – and the way through it is guided – only by the Master. The disciple cannot enter in of his own accord.

So, in the story, the Master Lithargoel comes forward to meet them in the guise of a physician, a healer, since a Master is a healer of souls sick from their involvement in and attachment to the world. And at first they do not recognize him for he is still wearing his garment of concealment. This garment is the physical body, for when the disciple looks at the physical form of the Master, he does not recognize who the Master really is – God, as the Word, in human form.

Only when the physical garment is removed and the soul ascends to and enters the Master's "city" inside, is the Master seen in his real form. As Lithargoel points out, this good man reveals himself only to a very few people, for "he himself is the son of a great king." He is the Son of God and only a few are destined to know it.

EPILOGUE

This short book is an introduction to the mystic literature of the ancient Middle East and particularly that which relates to our Western religious heritage: Christianity. It is also an expression of the timeless teachings of the mystics. Other books are planned in the same series.

Mystics come to this world to teach mankind how to resurrect themselves and find God within. The essence of their message is mystic experience through the practice of specific spiritual exercises, commonly known in the West as meditation. Their written or oral teachings are meant entirely to further that purpose, to encourage the souls of this world to seek Him – not through words, ritual or religion, but through inner experience.

The mind, however, having active and outward tendencies, is averse to meditation, especially of the kind taught by perfect Masters, for that sounds the death knell of its wayward nature. Only the direct, initiated disciples of a perfect Master know how to meditate in the way he instructs, and only they will receive the inner grace and blessings which keep them on that path. Consequently, after the departure of the mystic, if he appoints no successor, the knowledge and correct practice of meditation are soon forgotten, and within one or two generations all that remains are the written teachings.

For the true disciple of a Master, everything centres around the unspoken language of meditation. But for the followers of religion, the focus of attention becomes the verbal teachings. And therein lies a great difference. For the one is a meal, the other only a recipe. The one is travel, the other only a travel brochure. The one is an experience, the other only a description.

In the absence of meditation leading to inner mystic experience, the teachings alone, however sublime and inspiring they may be, are only a shell. And when people gather together in the name of these teachings but are not practising a technique of meditation whose purpose is to control the mind, the mind automatically takes over. Individuals interpret things differently, divisions set in, and there will always be some who set themselves up as authorities. A priesthood begins to develop, rituals and ceremonies creep in – and the road has begun that can lead to a religion.

So mystics come again and again, with the same perennial message and the same technique of meditation to teach. For the most part, they avoid the limelight and do not advertise. They have their own ways of drawing their allotted sheep into their fold. And all that a soul, asleep in Egypt, lost and wandering in the labyrinth of this world, can do, is to seek in all sincerity and earnestness. For it is, as the poem says, the Father who sends out the divine Letter, and the call to wakefulness, whenever He finds fit.

GLOSSARY

Mysticism requires the use of some definitive terminology. Since, in the West, the terms used in mysticism often possess a wide and general spread of meaning, certain key terms used in this book are defined below, together with other relevant entries.

Acts of John An early or mid second-century Christian composition, attributed to Leucius – supposedly a disciple of John, though nothing is known about him – and comprising a mixture of mystical discourses, sayings, hymns etc., and legendary stories.

Acts of Paul A mid second-century composition (*c.* AD 160) said by the church father Tertullian to have been written shortly before his time by a Christian presbyter of Asia in honour of Paul. However, the deception was discovered and the presbyter discharged from office. This is an interesting episode for it gives us an example of how some of these old writings came into existence. About half of the book is extant, mostly in a selection of Greek, Coptic, Syriac, Armenian, Slavonic and Latin fragments, demonstrating that the book had a wide range of popularity despite the fact that its origins were known to be dubious. The portion extant in the Syriac is entitled the *History of Thecla, the Disciple of Paul the Apostle*.

Acts of Peter A mid to late second century composition, purporting to relate some of the sayings, discourses and activities of Peter. The stories are frequently miraculous in nature – Peter, for example, once brings life to a dead herring – while the sayings and discourses are often mystical in content. The author is unknown, but is said by scholars to have modelled his style on the earlier *Acts of John*. Probably written in Greek, the majority of the extant text is found in a seventh century Latin manuscript, with another short episode in Coptic, though a large portion – perhaps one third, more or less – seems to be missing.

Acts of Peter and the Twelve Apostles A short tractate from the Nag Hammadi library in which Peter and the twelve apostles are set as pseudo-historical characters in a mystic allegory concerning a pearl merchant. In the story, the pearl merchant is revealed as Jesus.

Acts of Thomas A second or third century Christian composition of unknown authorship, comprising strange tales and mystic discourses, purporting to be a history of the apostle Thomas in India. *The Robe of Glory* is to be found among its confused, though largely mystical, contents. The *Acts of Thomas* and the *Acts of John* were adopted by the followers of Mani during the fourth century.

Allogenes A fictional, revelational discourse from the Nag Hammadi library, in which the central character Allogenes receives a mystic revelation of the inner realms of creation, recording the experience for the benefit of his 'son', Messos. Such 'apocalypses' or 'revelations' were a common literary type of ancient times, written for a variety of purposes, and of which there are many examples, one of them being the *Book of Revelation* in the New Testament.

 The name Allogenes means 'stranger,' 'alien', or 'one of another race', alluding to the soul, incarnate in this world, who feels like a stranger in a foreign land – a point of reality surrounded by an ocean of illusion or unreality.

apocrypha A class of ancient literature specifically excluded from the canonical or accepted scriptures. Hence, particularly, the *Old Testament Apocrypha* and the *New Testament Apocrypha*, each being a wide and diffuse body of literature.

Aramaic An ancient Semitic language of the Middle East, still spoken in parts of Syria and Lebanon. The language of Aram (Syria) in the fifth century BC, it spread to become the *lingua franca* of the Persian Empire. *See also* **Syriac**.

astral plane, realm, region or world The realm lying between the physical universe and the causal region. A world of the greater Mind, beguiling, fascinating and mostly blissful. The heavens of most religious aspirations are located here. In this region, the inclinations of the mind are immediately manifested as astral forms. The subtle, materio-mental energies of the astral region are formed from above and act as the blueprint for the physical universe.

There are degrees of subtlety and purity within the astral realm and souls automatically find their own level, according to their own mental propensities. The lowest areas of the astral world include the hells described by mystics and by many religions. It is here that the hellish tendencies which dominate individuals during their lifetime become a subtle, astral reality for them, as in dreams and nightmares. Similarly, purer minds may find a place in some astral heaven. But sooner or later the soul again takes birth in the physical universe, according to the physical attachments, tendencies and entanglements of the individual mind. Many souls simply take another birth, as soon as the previous one is ended.

Assumption of the Virgin An ancient legend found in many forms and languages, comprised of miraculous events and sayings centred around the later life and passing of Mary, the mother of Jesus. Its date and language of composition are very much a matter of scholarly debate.

Babel An ancient city, probably Babylon, where, according to the legend found in *Genesis 11:1–10*, the people built a tower in order to reach God. Their efforts, however, were confounded when Jehovah caused them all to speak different languages. The correct interpretation of this story is almost certainly intended to be allegorical. *See also* **Genesis**.

baptism An experience of initiation, regeneration or dedication, commonly used in referring to the Christian religious rite. Esoterically, the highest mystic baptism is initiation by a perfect Master, a re-tuning of the soul to the Word of God. *See also* **initiation**.

Bar Daisan or **Bardesanes** *c.* AD 155–233. A Syrian mystic, about whom little is known. Said to have been born in Edessa on the banks of the river Daisan and thought by some scholars to have been the author of *The Robe of Glory*.

causal plane, realm, region or **world** The highest region of the Mind; the region of the Universal Mind; the source of illusion; a blissfully intoxicating realm comprising the finest mental essences or energies, the seed or blueprint forms of time, space, causation and duality as we experience them in dense, crystallized manifestation in the physical universe. *See also* **astral plane, Mind, physical universe, Universal Mind.**

Christ From the Greek *Khristos* and Latin *Christus*, meaning, 'anointed one', being a translation of the Hebrew *Mashiah* or *Messiah*. Mystically, a term used for one anointed by God, a perfect Master.

Coptic An Afro-Asian language descended from ancient Egyptian but written in the Greek alphabet. Coptic dropped out of use as a spoken language in the sixteenth century, surviving only in the Coptic church. It is the language of the Nag Hammadi library, where it also contains many Greek words.

Dialogue of the Saviour One of the Nag Hammadi tractates, very poorly preserved in many places, seeming to be a record of a conversation between Jesus and some of his disciples, notably Mary, Judas and Matthew, and dating from the first century. The contents are mystical in nature. Since this writing must have travelled through several centuries, braved many copyists and editors, and have undergone a number of translations even before the Nag Hammadi papyrus was copied out in the fourth century, it is quite possible that its origins were in notes taken of one of the many conversations Jesus must have had with his disciples.

Divine Light The inner, mystic light experienced by the soul on its journey in the higher realms.

Divine Music or **Divine Sound** The inner, mystic sound of the Word, heard by the soul on its inner journey, and responsible for drawing the soul back to God.

Egypt An ancient, north-eastern African country, often used in the past by mystics of the Middle East as a symbol of slavery and exile in the physical universe.

Exegesis on the Soul An allegorical tractate from the Nag Hammadi library which tells the story of the pure and virgin soul leaving the Father and descending to this world. Here, she becomes attached to the things and people of the world, symbolized by her giving her love to all and sundry, becoming a prostitute. Realizing, ultimately, that no love of this world will last, she prays to the Father for help. The Father therefore sends to her a divine bridegroom, a Master, and cleansing herself in the mystic bridal chamber inside, she inwardly unites with him. In this way, she is "brought out of the land of Egypt", made pure and virginal once again, returning to her divine Father.

Genesis The first of the five books (the *Pentateuch*) attributed to Moses, common to the Bible of both Judaism and Christianity. Jewish and other mystics throughout the ages have commented that *Genesis* is a mystic allegory, not to be taken literally. Moreover, the text, as it has come down to us over a period spanning several thousand years, is understood from scholarly research to be corrupt in many places. Many changes, additions and deletions have been made over the course of its history and our present English translations have been made by those who did not recognize its mystical character. Amongst the oldest manuscripts available, there are a number of recensions (versions) available, pointing to the diversity which arises in almost all ancient literature.

gnostics A name given by scholars to any of a wide variety of mystics, or mystically-minded persons, who are characterized by the understanding that there exists a mystic or revealed knowledge (gnosis) by which all things can be known, especially the nature of the Self, God and all things of His creation. Hence, **gnosticism**.

gnosis Literally, knowledge, in particular mystic knowledge – an inner, revealed knowledge of God and the workings of His inner creation; an understanding which stems from direct mystic experience rather than intellectual analysis.

God The primal, self-existent Being and source of everything. *Also called* the **Father**, the **Lord**, **Ocean of Being**, **Universal Consciousness**, the **Source**, the **Supreme Being** and by many other names throughout the world.

God-realization The state of consciousness of a soul that has completely merged back into God and has come to know through experience that He is the ultimate Reality and source of all that is. Such a one may also, but not necessarily, be appointed to perform the duties of a perfect Master.

Gospel According to Saint John A late first or early second century Christian composition, written in erudite Greek, comprising spiritual discourses and stories concerning Jesus, some miraculous. Though attributed to the apostle John, scholars do not generally consider that he could have been the author of this fine Greek document, written between sixty and ninety years after the death of Jesus.

It is noteworthy that this gospel, like that according to St Mark, contains no nativity or virgin birth stories. In fact, the oldest versions of St Mark's gospel contain no resurrection stories either, and the last chapter of St John is also known to be a later addition. Many early Christians, especially those of a mystical inclination, did not believe in the virgin birth, nor in a physical resurrection of the body.

Our earliest complete manuscripts of this gospel date from the fourth and fifth centuries.

Gospel According to Saint Matthew A late first or early second century Christian composition, written in Greek by an unknown hand, around AD 75 or later, and attributed to the apostle Matthew. Writing in the name of a famous or even legendary character was common practice in ancient times and did not necessarily imply forgery, although in some cases this was undoubtedly the intention. According to scholarly analysis, this gospel is a compilation from a number of sources, one of which ('Q') – now lost – consisted of a collection of some of the sayings of Jesus. This source document of Jesus's sayings was also used by Luke, explaining the often word for word correspondence between these two gospels.

From its contents and style, the writer is normally presumed by scholars to have been Judaeo-Christian in outlook. It is clear, for example, that one of the writer's intentions was to prove, by frequent quotation from the Jewish scriptures, that Jesus was the Jewish Messiah. These quotations, however, are always taken out of their original context and sometimes edited to fit the writer's intended meaning and belief. Additionally, the source of some of these scriptural 'quotations' has yet to be traced.

Like all the New Testament documents, our earliest complete manuscripts date from the fourth and fifth centuries and there is every reason to believe that editorial changes, perhaps considerable, were made during its early history by those of 'orthodox' belief. This is consistent with the common fate of almost all ancient manuscripts, each one of which was individually hand-copied, providing ample opportunity for editorial 'adjustment', according to the beliefs and prejudices of the copyist or his employer.

Gospel of the Egyptians A tractate from the Nag Hammadi library, actually entitled the *Holy Book of the Great Invisible Spirit*. It tells the familiar story of creation by the Word, the "self-begotten" emanation of the Father, which creates everything, and appearing in the physical universe as the saviour, Jesus – a personification, in the thought of the writer, of the great Saviour, Seth. Emphasis is placed upon a mystic baptism, in particular a baptism of the "five seals" in "Living Water" or a "Spring of Truth".

Gospel of the Hebrews The lost gospel of the early Judaeo – Christians, also called the Nazarenes or Nazoraeans, but known to some of the early Christian fathers, including Jerome. It was said to have closely resembled our existing *Gospel According to St Matthew*, but contained some significant differences.

Gospel of Philip A miscellaneous collection, of uncertain date, of aphorisms, short comments, parables, discourses and so on, frequently of a mystical nature and evidently from the Christian tradition. The unknown author states that those who believe in a virgin birth and the resurrection of the dead bodies, either of themselves or of Jesus, are "in error". Philip is the only apostle named in it, and then on only one occasion. The title at the end of the book is presumed to have been derived from this single reference. One of the Nag Hammadi tractates.

Gospel of Thomas A collection of the sayings of Jesus discovered in the Nag Hammadi library. Before the Nag Hammadi find, this gospel was known only from a number of Greek fragments found amongst the rubbish heaps of ancient Oxyrhynchus in Egypt, and about whose origins scholars had advanced many theories, most of which turned out to be wrong. Like the lost source of Jesus's sayings ('Q'), used by the compilers of the gospels according to both Luke and Matthew, the *Gospel of Thomas* preserves some of the original sayings and parables of Jesus, and dates from the first century. The emphasis of these sayings is on finding the kingdom of Heaven within oneself.

greater Mind *See* **Mind.**

Hippolytus Generally thought to have been a Bishop of Portus, a harbour of Rome on the mouth of the river Tiber. His dates are uncertain, but he seems to have lived during the latter half of the second and early part of the third centuries. He has become well known for his work, *Refutation of all Heresies*, which castigates all other systems of thought and religion, especially 'deviant' Christian beliefs. This book was thought lost until a single Greek manuscript was found in the Greek monastery of Mount Athos in 1842. He was a disciple of St Irenaeus, Bishop of Lyons, also famous for his similar work *Against Heresies*, upon which Hippolytus modelled his own work and derived much of his 'information'.

Holy Ghost or **Holy Spirit** *See* **Word.**

individual mind A drop or ray of the Universal Mind, with which every human is endowed. It contains the seeds of an individual's destiny and records the new impressions due to actions and desires performed in the present life, as well as providing the characteristics of memory, intellect, discrimination, thought, emotion, personality, ego or identity, instinct and so on. *Also called* **human mind** or **physical mind.**

initiation A rite, ritual or experience by which an individual is accepted into a particular community. Esoterically, the highest mystic initiation has no ritualistic or sectarian aspects, but is the practical instruction of the individual into the techniques of meditation and the inner mystic connection or re-tuning of the soul to the Word of God. This can only be performed by a perfect Master, who takes up his abode within the disciple or initiate at that time, in his radiant or astral form. From that moment, also, the administration of the future destiny of the soul, its release from the realms of the Mind and its return to God are in the hands of the perfect Master. *See also* **baptism.**

Jerome AD ?347–?420. A Christian monk and scholar who produced the Latin translation of the Bible known as the Vulgate. This he accomplished, partly by translation from the original languages and partly by revising already existing Latin translations.

Jesus A mystic of Jewish birth, born *c.* 4 BC, who taught the path of the Word and in whose name the Christian religion has been formed.

karma The law of the greater Mind by which souls, under the influence of their individual minds are brought back into the labyrinth of birth and death. It is an automatic and natural law of cause and effect which exacts strict justice rather than mercy and forgiveness. The record of karma is held within the Mind as the impressions in seed form of all thoughts, actions and desires ever entertained or performed by an individual. Karma can be categorized as being of three kinds:

1. **Destiny karma** – the events of life which are fixed at the time of birth and which have to be undergone. They are the effects, good and bad, of previous actions, thoughts and desires from previous lives. Destiny is etched or pre-programmed into the complex fabric of our human mind and is outwardly expressed from there, over the course of a lifetime.

2. **New karma** – new actions and desires, performed or entertained in the present life, which become seeds or mental impressions for the destiny of future lives.

3. **Stored karma** – in one lifetime, an individual may gather more new karma than can be paid off in just one future life. Any balance of this 'unused' karma goes into 'storage'. Over the span of aeons, this store of karma becomes a great weight upon the soul, keeping it bound to the wheel of birth and death. This continues indefinitely, until the soul has the good fortune to meet a Master who has come from beyond the realm of karma and has the power to release souls from the Mind, by taking on responsibility for the payment of this vast debt.

Karma also means 'sins' and, from a mystic point of view, the 'forgiveness of sins' actually means help and guidance in the clearing of this great mountain of stored karma by a contemporary, living Master who is divinely qualified and appointed to do so. Such a Master inwardly connects or re-tunes the soul to the Creative Word or Logos – which is the real Master. It is the absorption of the mind and soul in the sound and light of the Creative Word which cleanses it of all past karmas and ultimately draws it back to God, beyond the realm of Mind and illusion. A perfect Master also pays off much of the karma of his initiates, either on his own body or out of the wealth of his own meditation. He can thus be said to ransom his disciples from the power of the Mind (Satan).

left hand path *See* **right hand path.**

light form of the Master The radiant, astral form of a perfect

Master, met by the initiate upon the threshold of the astral regions. This form, like the physical form, is a personification of the Word.

Living Water *See* **Word.**

Logos See **Word.**

Mandaeans A gnostic sect of Jewish origin that migrated to Mesopotamia in pre-or early Christian times. Surviving, until the middle of the present century as the last remaining gnostic sect, they lived in the marshlands of Iran and Iraq. Due to political conditions and the influence of the modern world, their present status is unsure. The Mandaeans acknowledge John the Baptist and many other mystics as having been Saviours or living Masters in their respective times. The earliest Mandaeans were vegetarian and drank no alcohol.

Mani AD ?215–?277. A Mesopotamian or Persian mystic whose ministry stretched from Rome to India, perhaps even China. The followers of the Manichaean religion which formed after his departure were greatly persecuted by the Christians wherever the two came into contact.

Messiah *See* **Christ.**

Mind or **mind** A general term, sometimes referring to the *individual* or *human mind*, sometimes to the *Universal Mind* and sometimes to any or all aspects of the Mind as it is found within the *three worlds of the Mind*. The higher aspects of the Mind, lying between the individual mind and the Universal Mind are also referred to as the *greater Mind*. Mind, when spelt with a capital 'M', refers to aspects above the individual mind. With a small 'm', it refers to the individual or human mind.

mysticism The study and practice of philosophies and techniques leading to the ascent of the soul and mind from the physical body. The highest mystical experience is the union of the soul with God. Hence, a mystic is one who is able to leave his body whilst still living, and the highest mystic is one who has attained God-realization.

Nag Hammadi Library A rare find of twelve gnostic codices or leather-bound, papyrus books, discovered in December 1944 by two Egyptian farmers in the Nag Hammadi region of upper Egypt. Containing a total of fifty-two gnostic tractates, they have become our most important literary source for the understanding of gnosticism. Amongst the many other conclusions that can be drawn from this find, it is clear that there were significant groups of early Christians who held that Jesus had been a great mystic and Saviour. Many of them expressed a belief in reincarnation, indicating that salvation was the release of the soul from birth and death and its subsequent return to God. Some of the tractates may even have been first written down in the time of Jesus, representing an earlier witness to what Jesus really taught than many things in the New Testament. The actual Nag Hammadi codices date from the second half of the fourth century. Written in Coptic, though almost certainly translated from the Greek, these tractates were first published in English in 1977, as *The Nag Hammadi Library in English*.

Name of God *See* **Word**.

Nazara Literally, 'Truth'. The Hebrew word from which the term 'Nazarene' or 'Nazoraean' is derived, meaning a follower or seeker of mystic Truth.

Nazirutha A Mandaean term for mystic 'Truth', variously referring to the Word, mystic realization or enlightenment, and also to the universal mystic teachings.

Odes of Solomon A collection of forty-two mystic, and often ecstatic, devotional poems in praise of the Lord, the Word and the Master, thought to have originated during early Christian times, or perhaps previously. They contain literary images and mystical truths also found in Jewish Wisdom literature, as well as in Essene, Christian, Mandaean and Manichaean mystical writings. Extant in both Syriac and Greek, though exhibiting an undoubted Semitic influence, scholars are divided as to which was the original language.

Origen AD ?185–?254. A Christian teacher of Greek cultural background, born into a Christian family of Alexandria, where he took over the running of a school of Christianity whilst still a young man. Often credited as having been the first Christian theologian and with having introduced theology into the orthodox Christian religion, Origen often spoke of Christianity in terms derived from Greek mysticism and philosophy. He – and in particular, his belief in the pre-existence of the soul – were later anathematized at the Fifth Ecumenical Council in AD 553, though some scholars maintain that the proposed anathemas were never actually passed.

Paraphrase of Shem A revelational and narrative discourse found in the Nag Hammadi library, describing the ascent of the mystic Shem from the physical realm to the "height of the creation" – God, the infinite Light. There, leaving behind his "Universal garment" of light, he returns to earth as a Saviour. The tractate contains pronounced elements of Greek mystical expression.

perfect Master A God-realized soul who has been appointed both by the Lord (inside) and by his own Master (outside) to initiate souls by connecting them to the Word, thus taking them back to God. He is a personification of the Word: the Word made flesh. In early Christian times, a perfect Master was also called the **Living One, Standing One, Christ, Messiah, Son of God, Son of Man, Son of Truth, Apostle, Envoy, Messenger, Saviour, Redeemer, Deliverer, Baptist, Friend of God, Door, Pearl, Great Fisherman, Shepherd, Sower of the Seed, Merchant of God, Treasurer, Bridegroom, Helmsman** and so on.

physical universe The region of dense matter and crystallized physical forms, where Mind reigns supreme, though largely unrecognized, remaining concealed within forms. The realm in which the soul, under the influence of the mind's attractions and tendencies, takes birth in successive bodies, together with corresponding destinies, both of which accurately reflect the character of the individual mind. Often referred to by Jesus and by many other mystics as the 'prison', 'dungeon' or 'pit'. *See also* **individual mind**.

Pistis Sophia One of the earliest Coptic manuscripts to be discovered, the Askew Codex was bought by the British Museum from the heirs of Dr Askew in 1785. Much of its contents are taken up with the story of *Pistis Sophia*, which has come to be the title by which the whole codex is commonly referred. The codex is more correctly called, according to the inscription of the original scribes, *A Portion of the Books of the Saviour*. *Pistis*

Sophia (literally, 'Faith-Wisdom') tells the story of the soul descending to the physical realm and being rescued by the Saviour, Jesus.

In these *Books of the Saviour*, Jesus is in conversation with his disciples, discoursing, telling stories and answering questions. Frequent mention is made of the Treasury of Light, of the vestures or robes of the soul, of the inner realms and the inner mysteries, of baptism or initiation, of the five names of the five rulers, of the five trees, of the Great Name, of the seven Voices, of reincarnation and of much else besides.

radiant form of the Master *See* **light form of the Master.**

reincarnation The incarnation of a soul in successive physical bodies, human or otherwise, due to the influence, tendencies and involvements of the mind. *Also called* **transmigration** or **metempsychosis.** *See also* **karma.**

right hand path Refers to mystic ascent upon the Word, the path which leads back to God. Conversely, the *left hand path* refers to magic, psychism, spirit contact and other practices which keep an individual involved with the mind and, at best, can only take a soul into other areas of the Mind – release from birth and death not being attained.

There is also an esoteric or mystic significance to the right and left hand paths. In simple terms, it can be said that the Word moves out from God, creates the creation and then returns to Him. The downward, creative current of the Word constitutes the left hand path. Consequently, even contact with the sound and light on the left hand side will ultimately bring a soul back into this world, keeping it within the creation, particularly the worlds of the Mind.

To return to God a soul must be in contact with the sound and light of the positive, right hand current – the current which ascends back to God.

salvation The release of the soul from the realms of the Mind. This implies both Self-realization as well as release from the wheel of birth and death on the physical plane. *Also called* **redemption** or **liberation.** Hence, a perfect Master is also called a **Saviour,** a **Redeemer** or an **Emancipator.**

Satan The 'devil' of Muslim, Jewish and Christian belief. A term predating Christianity. Whatever the term may have come to mean in the popular mind, mystics refer to Satan as the Negative Power, the power or lord who rules the Universal Mind and all the realms that lie within the Mind. This includes the physical, astral and causal realms. From a mystic point of view, all the faculties or powers of the human mind, positive or negative, are therefore aspects of Satan, but it is necessary to divest the mind of the conditioned, religious understanding of the term, in order to appreciate this. *Also called* the **Adversary**, the **Enemy**, the **Prince of Darkness**, the **Prince of the World**, the **Devil**, the **Wicked One**, the **Sinner**, the **Serpent**. *See also* **Universal Mind**.

Self-realization The mystic knowledge of the soul that it is pure soul, only attained when the soul gains release from all aspects of the Mind, on rising above the Universal Mind. This is an inner mystic experience, not an intellectual or psychological thought process.

single eye The point of focus of the mind and soul in the human form, lying slightly above and between the two physical eyes. It has no real physical location, but lies in an altogether more subtle plane. It is here that the soul and mind, experienced as the attention, can be concentrated, thereby withdrawing all consciousness from the body below the eyes. Subsequently, the soul and mind go further within, passing through the gates of death while still living in the physical body. *Also called* **door of the house, eye centre, third eye, tenth gate, door of brightness**.

Son of God The primal emanation or 'son' of God the Father, also known as the Word or Logos. Also, the personification of this power in the person of a perfect Master. *See also* **perfect Master**.

Sophia of Jesus Christ A Christian overwriting of the discourse entitled *Eugnostos the Blessed*, both of which were found in the Nag Hammadi library. Possibly dating from the first century, the text is deeply gnostic in character, purporting to be a discourse given by Jesus to his disciples after his resurrection, though "not in his previous form, but in the invisible spirit".

Part of the tractate's interest lies in the ability to observe the Christianizing of a previously extant mystic document. Both tractates are concerned with a description of the grand hierarchy of the inner creation and the fall of man into this world. A Saviour is therefore sent on a mission of redemption. In the *Sophia of Jesus*

Christ, the Saviour is Jesus. In *Eugnostos the Blessed*, the name
of the Saviour is not mentioned.

soul A term used throughout the ages in reference to many
psychological and spiritual aspects of a human being. Mystically,
the soul is said to be a drop of the divine ocean, constituting the
true Self and innermost essence.

Syriac A Semitic language, a dialect of Aramaic spoken in Syria and
the Middle East during and before the early Christian era. Just as
Greek was the international language of the West in ancient
times, Syriac was the *lingua franca* further to the East, becoming
the language of the Eastern church. It still survives as the language
of those churches retaining the old Syriac liturgies. *See also*
Aramaic.

Teachings of Silvanus A tractate from the Nag Hammadi library
which demonstrates that the teachings of Jesus were compatible
with the best of both Jewish and Greek mystical tradition. The
author presents the mystic teachings of Jesus in the manner of a
discourse, using both Greek and Jewish mystical terms, since they
were no doubt a part of the background of both his audience and
himself. The purity of the mystical expression in this tractate is
such that it could possibly have been written by a direct disciple
of Jesus.

Testimony of Truth A forceful discourse from the Nag Hammadi
library which points out that no one can reach God unless he is
prepared to give up all other attachments to the world, dedicating
himself wholeheartedly to the task of God-realization. The author
lays great emphasis on baptism into the "life-giving Word", also
advising his readers not to expect any resurrection of the physical
body.

Thought of Norea One of the shortest tractates in the Nag
Hammadi library, containing only fifty-two lines of text. An
untitled text, it shows evidence of both Jewish and Greek mystical
expression. God is represented as the Primal Thought, at one with
the "Voice of Truth, upright Nous, untouchable Logos and
ineffable Voice". The tractate is of particular interest for it
demonstrates that the Greek term 'Nous', usually translated by
scholars as 'Mind', as well as the term 'Logos', usually translated
as 'Reason' or 'Word', (as in the beginning of St John's gospel),

were both used by mystics to refer to the same creative power.

three worlds of the Mind The three worlds ruled by the Universal Mind, *viz.* the physical, astral and causal realms.

tractate A short treatise or tract, especially of a religious, moral or spiritual nature.

Treatise on the Resurrection A short tractate from the Nag Hammadi library, being a letter addressed to a certain Rheginos on the true and spiritual meaning of resurrection.

Trimorphic Protennoia Literally, 'the Three-Formed [Divine] Primal Thought'. A tractate from the Nag Hammadi library which appears to have been overwritten by both Sethian and Christian editors. It tells the story of the divine descent of the Word or the Voice into this world, as the Son and Saviour. Initiation is also described as being immersed in the "Water of Life" and receiving the "five seals", after which the soul becomes "a Light in Light".

Universal Mind The power that rules the three worlds of the Mind: the physical, astral and causal realms. *Also called* **Satan, Babel, Negative Power, Prince of Darkness,** the **Enemy,** the **Adversary, Prince of the World, Demiurge, Beelzebub, Belial, Ialdabaoth,** and by many other names throughout the world.

Voice of God *Also called* the **Voice, Silent Voice, Visible Voice, Voice of Truth, Real Voice, Ineffable Voice, Unreproducible Voice, Hidden Voice.** *See* **Word.**

Word or Creative Word The primal, creative power of God which underlies all creation, within and without. *Also called* the **Logos, Nous, Name of God, Thought of God, Wisdom, Hidden Wisdom, Voice of God, Sound Current, Audible Life Stream, Divine Music, Divine Sound, Music of the Spheres, Holy Spirit, Holy Ghost, Comforter, Living Waters, Radiant Waters, Immeasurable Spring, Spring of Truth, Wellspring,** and by many other names throughout the world.

Zostrianos One of the longest tractates in the Nag Hammadi library, though unfortunately the codex containing it has suffered such great damage that there are holes in the papyrus on almost every page. The tractate tells the story of how a certain Zostrianos, yearning for a true understanding of spiritual truths, becomes deeply depressed and gloomy, contemplating whether or not to commit suicide by delivering himself to the "wild beasts of the desert for a violent death". At this psychological moment, his yearnings are answered and he receives a vision from an angel and is taken up, out of his physical body, and shown the workings of the entire inner creation. This literary, and almost certainly fictional, framework provides the author with a means, common enough in those times, of describing the inner regions of creation, as he understands them. A considerable element of Greek mystical expression and terminology is found in this tractate.

ABBREVIATIONS

In the main text, the following abbreviations have been used (*See* Bibliography for full details):

AAA   *Apocryphal Acts of the Apostles*, W.R. Wright
ANT   *The Apocryphal New Testament*, M.R. James
AOT   *The Apocryphal Old Testament*, ed. H.E.D. Sparks
B   *Brahman*, W.B. Henning
CPM   *The Canonical Prayerbook of the Mandaeans*, E.S. Drower
GS   *The Gnostic Scriptures*, Layton Bentley
GVMAG   *The Great Vohu Manah and the Apostle of God*, Geo Widengren
MHCP   *The Manichaean Hymn-Cycles in Parthian*, Mary Boyce
ML   *Manichaean Literature*, J.P. Asmussen
MM   *Mani and Manichaeism*, G. Widengren
MMP   *On Mithra in the Manichaean Pantheon*, Mary Boyce.
NHL   *The Nag Hammadi Library in English*, ed J.M. Robinson
SA   *The Secret Adam*, E.S. Drower
SCMP   *Studies in the Coptic Manichaean Psalm-Book*, Torgny Säve-Söderbergh
SOL   *Sayings of Our Lord*, B.P. Grenfell and A.S. Hunt
SP   *Sadwes and Pesus*, Mary Boyce

BIBLIOGRAPHY

APOCRYPHAL LITERATURE

The Apocryphal Acts of the Apostles, translated from the Syriac by W. Wright; Williams and Norgate, Edinburgh, 1871.

The Apocryphal New Testament, translated from the Greek by M.R. James; Oxford University Press, New York; first edition 1924, corrected 1953, edition used 1989.

The Apocryphal Old Testament, translated by various scholars, edited by H.E.D. Sparks; Oxford University Press, Oxford, 1985.

Odes and Psalms of Solomon, translated from the Syriac by J. R. Harris; Cambridge University Press, Cambridge, 1911.

Odes of Solomon, translated from the Syriac by J. H. Charlesworth; Oxford University Press, Oxford, 1973.

Odes of Solomon, translated from the Syriac by J.H. Bernard; Cambridge University Press, Cambridge, 1912.

Odes of Solomon, translated from the Syriac by J.A. Emerton, in *The Apocryphal Old Testament*, translated by various scholars, edited by H.E.D. Sparks; Oxford University Press, Oxford, 1985.

Sayings of Our Lord, from an Early Greek Papyrus, B.P. Grenfell and A.S.Hunt; Henry Frowde, London, 1897.

CANONICAL LITERATURE AND NEW TESTAMENT COMMENTARIES

The Bible – Authorized King James Version, Oxford University Press, London and Toronto, undated.

Light on Saint Matthew, Maharaj Charan Singh; Radha Soami Satsang Beas, P.O. Dera Baba Jaimal Singh, near Beas, Amritsar, Punjab 143204, India, 1978.

Light on Saint John, Maharaj Charan Singh; Radha Soami Satsang Beas, P.O. Dera Baba Jaimal Singh, near Beas, Amritsar, Punjab 143204, India, 1985.

GENERAL MYSTICISM

The Path of the Masters, Dr Julian Johnson; Radha Soami Satsang Beas, P.O. Dera Baba Jaimal Singh, near Beas, Amritsar, Punjab 143204, India; first published 1939, revised edition 1965.

GNOSTIC LITERATURE

Against Heresies, Bishop Irenaeus, translated by A. Roberts and W.H. Rambaut; T. & T. Clark; Edinburgh, 1868.

The Complete Echoes from the Gnosis, G.R.S. Mead; originally published in eleven short volumes by the Theosophical Publishing Society, London and Benares, 1906-1908; present edition edited by Stephen Ronan, Chthonios Books, Hastings, England, 1987.

Fragments of a Faith Forgotten, G.R.S. Mead; first published by the Theosophical Publishing Society, London and Benares, 1906. Present edition reprinted by Health Research, Mokelumne Hill, California 95245, USA, 1976.

The Gnostic Scriptures, translated by Bentley Layton, with annotations and introductions. SCM Press Ltd., London, 1987.

The Hymn of the Soul contained in the Syriac Acts of Thomas, re-edited with an English translation by A.A. Bevan; Cambridge University Press, Cambridge, 1897.

The Nag Hammadi Library in English, edited by J.M. Robinson; third, completely revised edition, E.J. Brill, Leiden, the Netherlands, 1988.

Pistis Sophia, A Gnostic Gospel, G.R.S. Mead; Garber Communications, New York, 1984, being a reprint of Mead's 1921 edition.

Refutation of All Heresies, Bishop Hippolytus, translated by S.D.F. Salmond; T. & T. Clark, Edinburgh, 1868.

MANI AND MANICHAEISM

Brahman, W.B. Henning, in 'Transactions of the Philological Society', pp. 112–13, London, 1944.

The Great Vohu Manah and the Apostle of God, Geo Widengren; Uppsala, Sweden, 1945.

Mani and Manichaeism, Geo Widengren; Weidenfeld and Nicholson, London, 1961.

The Manichaean Hymn-Cycles in Parthian, translated by Mary Boyce; Oxford University Press, London and New York, 1954.

Manichaean Literature, Jes P. Asmussen; Scholars' Facsimiles & Reprints Inc, Delmar, New York, 1975.

On Mithra in the Manichaean Pantheon, Mary Boyce, in *A Locust's Leg: Studies in Honour of S.H. Taqizadeh*, edited by W.B. Henning and Ehsan Yarshater; Percy Lund, Humphries & Co., London, 1962.

Sadwes and Pesus, Mary Boyce; in 'Bulletin of the School of Oriental and African Studies', vol. 13 no. 4, 1951.

Studies in the Coptic Manichaean Psalm-Book, Torgny Säve-Söderbergh; Uppsala, Sweden and W. Heffer & Sons, Cambridge, 1949.

MANDAEAN LITERATURE

The Canonical Prayerbook of the Mandaeans, translated with notes by E.S. Drower; E.J. Brill, Leiden, the Netherlands, 1959.

The Secret Adam, E.S. Drower; Oxford University Press, Oxford, 1960.

INDEX